Buried Soul

A Story of Survival

Elfriede E. Wilde

Copyright 2017 Elfriede E. Wilde
4206 Monroe Drive
Texarkana, TX 75503
(903) 223-8075

All rights reserved. No part of this book may be reproduced in any form or by any means, electronic or mechanical, including photocopying, or by any information storage and retrieval system, without written permission from the author.

Some names have been changed to protect the privacy of the individuals

Copyright for title page granted
by Stuttgart Stadtarchiv, Stuttgart, Germany
ISBN: 978-0-9984069-4-7

Published by Shari Parker Publishing
2895 CR 3103
New Boston, Texas 75570
sharipar@yahoo.com
www.shariparkerpublishingandprinting.com
903-933-6273

Dedicated to my friends
Who survived the war with me
And to those who did not

The title page shows St. Leonhard's Church in Stuttgart, after the destruction in the war.

The church was first documented in 1337 as a small chapel. After the bombing on July 25, 1944, the statue of Jesus on the Cross with Mary and Mary Magdalene was left standing among the rubble.

"This is a sign of God," some people whispered as they walked by the statue. They were afraid to say it out loud. They might have been arrested.

Table of Contents

Preface.. 6
Acknowledgements................................ 8

Chapter One
Life Before the War............................... 9
My First Boyfriend................................ 12
The Tagblatt Tower Paternoster   14
Other Childhood Memories................ 15
The Danube.. 16
Ahnenpass (Proof of Ancestry)   18

Chapter Two
Beginning of the War............................ 21
The First Air Raid Warning.................. 29
Aunt Karoline's House.......................... 35
The Train... 37
Education and Physical Fitness   40
Night of Horror...................................... 44
Stuttgart September 1944................... 49
My Mother's Dreams............................ 50
The Last Days of the War..................... 51
Volkssturm (Militia).............................. 80
The Cross... 83
A Hero.. 84

Chapter Three
New Beginnings..................................... 91
Puppets and Flowers with Roots........ 101

Hunger..	*104*
My Apple Hat.....................................	*105*
Wilhelmsglueck..................................	*107*
The Pig...	*110*
New Money..	*112*
Christmas Eve in Russia.....................	*113*
Scotland	120
The Switchboard Girls from................ Burgholzhof	123
James..	127
The Bible...	161
The Memorial......................................	165

Chapter Four
Texas...	168
Nehemiah..	174

PREFACE

I belong to the generation of children who grew up in Stuttgart, Germany, during World War II. Not many of us are living today. I feel that it is important to tell our stories, stories that many people today do not understand or do not believe.

We lived through the war, through hunger, through the death of friends and through the destruction of our beautiful city. We survived because we helped each other survive. We dug ourselves out from the rubble, and we formed friendships for life.

There was no elbow society. We respected each other, encouraged each other and shared our meager belongings. We will never forget Hitler's dictatorship. Many of us suppressed the memory for years, but we never forgot.

After the war, books were written about Hitler. The books described how he planned to conquer the world. Details were published about Germany's destroyed cities and about the Holocaust. Statistics about the war vary. Some military historians claim that about 2.44 million civilians were killed in Germany during the war. Some say the worldwide loss of lives was between fifty and seventy million people.

However, people wrote very little about how they lived and survived during the war and the difficult years that followed. The memories were too painful. Nearly fifty years passed until more eyewitnesses were able to share their experiences and put them down on paper.

After I married again in 1995, my husband Harold Wilde shared some of his Korean war experiences with me. Nobody in his family was interested in hearing about it. He encouraged me to talk about the things that happened to me. Our talks were a healing process for both of us. A few years later, I was finally able to write about it. When I visit Germany, I see my old friends. Our group is getting small. We reminisce about things we experienced. We will always appreciate things our children, grandchildren and great-grandchildren take for granted, things like soap, chocolate, elegant shoes or sleeping in a warm bed on a cold winter night. I pray that they will never, never have to go through a war, watch their friends perish and see their world disappear.

ACKNOWLEDGMENTS

I want to express my gratitude to my beloved husband Harold Wilde, who encouraged me to compile my notes, letters and memories to write this book. I wish he could have lived long enough to see the completed work.

Special thanks go to my friends Susan Boyle and Daniel Brower, who reviewed part of my manuscript, and to my friend Janet Buchanan, whose continuous encouragement made it possible for me to complete this book.

Sarah George had helpful suggestions, which I appreciated. Most of all I thank David Quinnelly for his help with my computer programs. Without his expertise this book would not have been printed.

CHAPTER ONE

LIFE BEFORE THE WAR

I was born on Christmas Eve. I always envied my friends who had birthday parties during the year and could invite the neighborhood children. I never had a birthday party. My mother was always too busy during that time of year. I hated it when I received a birthday gift wrapped in Christmas paper. Until this day, my very best friends are those who send a Christmas card and a separate birthday card.

Christmas in Germany starts with Advent Sunday, the fourth Sunday before Christmas. Nearly every family has an Advent wreath woven from pine boughs and decorated with red or gold ribbons and four candles.

My family usually gathered at my grandparents' home on the afternoon of the first Advent Sunday. Grandmother served coffee and her famous Christmas Springerle cookies, baked in wooden molds that Grandpa had carved. My mother played the piano, and she and Grandmother sang Christmas carols. I still remember their beautiful voices, my grandmother's rich alto accompanied by my mother's clear, high soprano. I wish I had inherited their musical talents. Unfortunately, I cannot even carry a tune.

Then I was allowed, under close supervision, to light the first candle on the Advent wreath. This tradition was repeated for the next three Sundays. A new candle was lit every Sunday until all four candles announced that Christmas Eve was nearly here. My mother always purchased an Advent calendar with pictures that I could open, one picture a day until December 24.

On December 6th, St. Nicholas arrived, carrying a large sack with small presents for children who had been good. Hoping to find candy, cookies or a small toy the next morning, children put their shoes outside apartment doors, so he could leave a gift. Occasionally, St. Nicholas would check on a child in person. This happened to me once, and I remember how scared I was. After I was able to recite a poem, I received a small gift, and much to my relief St. Nicholas left to visit other children.

Christmas markets are part of Germany's history. They date back to the fifteenth century. People come from around the world to see them. The first Christmas market in Stuttgart was held in 1692 and is one of the largest in Europe. About two weeks before Christmas, my mother, my grandmother and I went to the Christmas Market at Market Square in the center of town. It was a fairytale land.

A huge Christmas tree was decorated with hundreds of golden lights, its branches reaching up into the sky. Vendors had set up their wares on tables in small tents or in booths. They offered everything a child or adult could imagine. Christmas decorations, hand-carved mangers, toys, crafts and food were displayed. Tantalizing smells of gingerbread, roasted nuts, Christmas cakes and cookies, dates, oranges and hot wine spiced with cinnamon and cloves wafted over the crowds. Choirs as well as single musicians played and sang Christmas carols. I was enchanted.

When the war started, things changed. A Christmas tree was still erected but without lights. Oranges and dates had disappeared, as well as many other foods. Still, people clung to the old tradition and tried to keep the Christmas spirit alive. Eventually, the bombings of the city stopped it all until after the war. In the 1970s, the Christmas Market began to look like a small village. Tables and tents made way for booths, many of them looking like small houses ablaze with Christmas lights. It has now become a tourist sensation. Busses bring in thousands of people to shop, eat and drink. Somehow, the enchantment of my childhood has turned into commercial success. Unlike the United States, the big celebration in Germany is on Christmas Eve. Even though stores and streets are decorated early with Christmas trees and other decorations, families usually do not put up the Christmas tree until the evening of December 24. The tree usually stays up until January 6th. I still follow this custom here at my home in America.

MY FIRST BOYFRIEND

Reinhold and I, Stuttgart, Summer 1932

His name was Reinhold. He had silver blonde hair cut into a pageboy. My mother said his name should have been Siegfried or Gunther because he looked like a child from the Song of the Nibelungs, a German epic poem from the Middle Ages. Our mothers were friends, and we often met in the park. I loved the park with its tall trees, birds singing and squirrels chasing each other up and down the tree trunks.

We sat on a gray sun-warmed stone bench, and Reinhold read to me from a magical book. He read about castles where kings and queens lived, about knights, princesses and fairies. Among the rustling of leaves, I could hear a faint whisper. For just a moment, I was sure I saw the fairies, their golden hair flying in the wind, their iridescent bodies dancing between the trees and vanishing behind the sun. I cannot remember Reinhold's mother's name, but even today when I think of her, I think of a bright light, a happy feeling and a mystery. I was convinced that she was one of the fairies who we believed visited the park, and that one day she had stayed behind.

Reinhold promised to always read fairy tales to me and protect me forever. One day he picked two dandelions in the park and gave one to me. My mother took a picture of us, each one holding a dandelion and Reinhold putting his arm protectively around my shoulders. This photo is one of the few that survived the war.

Fall came. Reinhold and I watched the leaves on the trees turn to brilliant colors of red, orange and golden yellow. The winds came and plucked at the leaves. It whirled them through the air, slowly at first in a graceful dance, then faster and faster, up and down. Their colors glowed like jewels in the sun, finally settling softly on the still warm earth. We had fun catching leaves and putting them in one of Reinhold's books to keep them forever, and we watched the butterflies who did not know yet that winter would be here soon.

One day Reinhold and his mother did not come to the park. Rains came and then storms, ripping the last clinging leaves from the branches, hurling them to the ground. The squirrels had gathered all the nuts they could find. My mother said they were hibernating somewhere in unseen shelters. The dandelions had stopped blooming. The park was desolate. The fairies had left. The first snow fell, putting a soft white blanket around my vanished magical summer. I never saw Reinhold again, and nobody picked dandelions for me anymore. All I have left is a picture of two children who believed in fairies and magic and lived in a world that was still whole.

THE TAGBLATT TOWER *PATERNOSTER*

When I grew up in Stuttgart we had no television, computers, cell phones or iPads to keep us busy. Not every family had a radio, and only a few private homes had a telephone. Still, we never ran out of things to do, and we always had fun. Traffic was light; so we played in the streets. We rode our scooters in the small park on Bismarck Square, where we also could splash in a terrific wading pool on hot summer days, or we roller-skated in front of St. Paulus Church.

We knew every family who lived on our street and on neighboring streets, and we felt safe. If necessary, we could call on every mother of a playmate for help, for instance if one of us slipped on horse droppings. There was always someone to put a band aid on a skinned knee to make us feel better. Parental supervision was light, which enabled us to sometimes wander farther from our neighborhood without any parents noticing. As long as we were home by the time the evening prayer bell chimed from the church, everything was all right.

On some occasions, we became bored with everyday games and wanted to do something more exciting. At such times, we went to the Tagblatt Tower, a six-story tower that housed the *Neue Stuttgarter Tagblatt*, Stuttgart's daily newspaper. The attraction of the tower was its elevator, a *Paternoster*. This elevator never stopped. The open compartments linked together and moved continuously on a circular belt.

To ride the elevator, we had to jump on while it was in motion and then jump off on the floor we wanted to go to. It was an exciting and daring adventure, and we loved it. If we were really brave, we would stay on the elevator until it reached the top floor. Then we had to duck down low or lay on the floor until the elevator started its downward trip on the other side.

Much later, I found out that *Paternoster* is also the name for the Lord's Prayer.

We were never caught on our downtown excursion. About 1942, the war was beginning to be felt more in Stuttgart, and our *Paternoster* trips ended. One day I told my mother about our *Paternoster* trips. She was horrified! I am sure that she and the other mothers would have prayed many a Lord's Prayer had they known about their children's adventures.

OTHER CHILDHOOD MEMORIES

Another exciting adventure always started when we heard the call of the *Scherenschleifer*, the scissor and knife sharpener, offering his services. Housewives brought their dull kitchen knives and sewing scissors to be sharpened. The *Scherenschleifer*'s sharpening wheel was mounted on a small cart with a hand-operated pump. As he turned the wheel, a small stream of water was pumped on the instrument to be sharpened. Sometimes my friends and I were allowed to hand the *Scherenschleifer* a knife or a pair of scissors or even to operate the pump. We watched his work with fascination.

Next came the rag and paper collector. He pulled a hand wagon through the streets and called "*Lumpen und Papier,*" which means rags and paper. The practice was actually very early recycling. Nothing was wasted if it could be reused. Once the war and the bombings started, these collections stopped. People hung onto every scrap of material; there was nothing to give away anymore.

THE DANUBE

She is called the "Blue" Danube, the mighty river that flows from Germany through Austria and Hungary, emptying into the Black Sea. Songs have been written about her. Poets and musicians were inspired by her beauty. One of the most famous was Johann Strauss who composed the "Blue Danube Waltz."

My mother and I often spent part of the summer in our apartment in Ulm, a town on the banks of the Danube. We lived a short walk from the river. My friends and I spent lazy days swimming and playing in the roped-off area by the river, while my mother sat on the bank in front of her easel, painting images of the old city wall, the cathedral and the river.

It was a hot August day. We were wading and playing in the roped-off area at the river's edge. Later, we never could remember who made the first dare to swim across the Danube. It was a crazy idea, birthed by sheer boredom. I looked up to where my mother who was busy with paints and brushes, completely absorbed in her work.

"Let's do it," one of my friends whispered.

Quietly, three of us swam under the ropes and out into

deeper waters. The others stayed behind, looking alarmed. Cool water caressed my skin. The sun spun golden circles around us. We swam hard for a while. The bank on the other side seemed far away. I turned on my back. Fleecy clouds slowly drifted across the sky. Swallows flew low over the water, predicting rain for the next day. The steeples of the nearby cathedral glinted golden in the afternoon sun. It was magic.

Suddenly, I heard shouts from the bank. My mother ran along the stone path at the water's edge, skirt flapping around her ankles, hair flying, a paintbrush waving wildly in the air.

"Come back here," she yelled. "Come back right now."

I turned back on my stomach. My friends were swimming close by. Two small fishing boats floated in the middle of the stream. The fishermen waved to us. We started to swim harder again toward the bank opposite from my mother, but the current was carrying us toward the New-Ulm Bridge downstream. About fifteen minutes later, we reached the bridge. We climbed out of the water, scrambled up the bank, and walked across the bridge, barefoot and in our bathing suits, ignoring people's stares. We entered the stone walk and there, looking like a giant statue, stood my mother. We were banished from the river for the rest of the summer.

Today, nobody swims across the Danube. Her beautiful waters have turned gray from pollution. A commission has been formed to bring her beauty back.

One of my mother's drawings of the Danube, Ulm 1943

AHNENPASS
Proof of Ancestry

Germany is the only country that once required its citizens to compile their genealogy for political reasons. Most countries today register birth, marriage and death, but people do not need to go back for generations.

Under Hitler's twelve-year reign, German citizens were required to compile a document called *Ahnenpass*. Literally translated, it means ancestor passport, but it was not a passport. It was a document that proved that a person was a true Aryan, not a Jew or gypsy or any other race.

The *Ahnenpass* consisted of forty-eight pages, not including Hitler's introductory remarks:
"The complete educational system of the state of the people must find its highest achievement in burning into the hearts and minds of the youth entrusted into our care

the reason for race and the feeling for race. No boy, no girl, shall leave school without having fully understood the reasons for this and the nature of pure blood. This will assure the preservation of the racial roots of our nation and through it, it will secure our cultural development."

Racial purity meant that only people of strictly Aryan origins could be granted privileges under German laws. Anyone not fitting into this pattern was a second-class citizen or was not even allowed German citizenship. The only way one could prove this purity was to compile a personal genealogy.

Everyone had to have an *Ahnenpass*, going back at least four generations to great-grandparents. Some occupations such as school teachers, journalists, publishers, army officers, policemen and all SS soldiers were required to check their backgrounds even further back. When I entered first grade in 1936, my parents had to submit an *Ahnenpass*.

All entries in the *Ahnenpass* had to be verified by officials. People had to go to the towns where their ancestors were born and visit churches and civil registrar offices, or request the information by mail. Entries from these records were copied into the *Ahnenpass* and verified with an official stamp, usually for a small fee.

When the bombing of German cities started in 1940, many cities and towns moved their original church and civil registry records to safe places. They were taken to small villages, salt mines, cellars in castles in the country, or other underground shelters. These records were extremely important to prove Aryan ancestry. As a result, not as many records were destroyed as many people think. The records lost were mostly in the country in small villages and happened during fighting in the last days of the war.

As soon as I could read, I read our *Ahnenpass* and imagined the lives of my ancestors. Some had unusual names, interesting occupations and lived in places I had never heard of. I wanted to know more about them, and thus my love for genealogy was born.

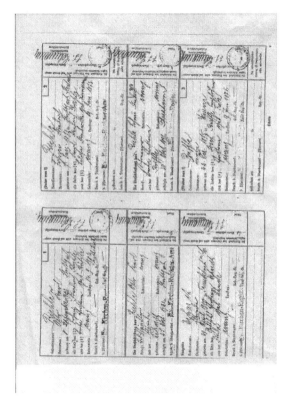

AHNENPASS

CHAPTER TWO

WAR
September 1, 1939 - May 7, 1945

BEGINNING OF THE WAR

On the morning of September 1, 1939, my mother turned on the radio. She put the breakfast dishes in the sink; then, in the early morning light, she set up her easel in the alcove. The dishes would have to wait. As she gathered her paints and brushes, a voice came over the air waves asking everyone to stand by. Adolf Hitler, the Fuehrer, was about to make an important announcement. Patriotic music gave way to the easy listening music she enjoyed. She waited.

Just the evening before friends had gathered at our house. They talked about Danzig and several incidents at the Polish border. Some thought that there might be war. My mother shivered. Surely not! She remembered her parents' stories about the war. It started in 1914, when she was about three years old.

Her father, a railroad employee, was drafted August 3, 1914, just three days after the war had started. He served with honor in the Railroad Company of the 121st Infantry Regiment and received the Iron Cross for bravery. Her mother Luise, like many other wives of railroad employees, immediately volunteered to fill one of the many spaces vacated by men.

Leaving her little girl in the care of an elderly neighbor, she donned black woolen pants and jackets and became a train conductor. Women did not wear pants in the early twentieth century. The railroad women were called "hussies" by some of their neighbors. Even so, they held their heads high and proudly wore their railroad uniforms.

Music from the radio still filled the room. It was interrupted every few minutes by an announcer. Hitler would speak any minute now. Would he declare war? No – that was not possible.

My mother recalled other stories her mother had told her. Food was scarce during World War I. Though forbidden by the government, people took trains to the country to buy milk, eggs, potatoes, flour and any food they could get from farmers. The trains were stopped often, and the food confiscated by government officials. Some people were convinced that these officials kept at least some of the food for themselves, but nobody could prove it.

One day Luise and one of her girlfriends were on a train coming back to Stuttgart from the country. Each carried nearly a gallon of milk in a metal jug covered with a lid. Suddenly the train shuddered, the wheels came to a screeching stop. They were near the station at the west end of town. Within seconds, policemen tore open the doors.

"Everybody out!" they yelled.

The passengers, mostly women, knew it meant their food would be confiscated. The policemen checked the train to make sure that everything edible was carried off. Lines formed. At the front of the lines sat men at small tables. Next to them stood large bins where the collected food items were deposited. There was no fine if the food was turned in, but anyone who refused was led away.

With heavy hearts, Luise and her friend stepped off the train, clutching their jugs tightly to their bodies. The two women made their way to the back of the longest line. They looked at each other, smiling faintly, then removed the lids from their jugs. They lifted them to their mouths and started drinking the milk that was supposed to be for their little children.

As their line moved forward, the women were still drinking. Before they reached the table, the jugs were empty. Not being used to such rich fare, the two women began to feel very sick. Luise reached the table first and promptly threw up, missing the table and a stunned man by inches. She wiped her mouth with her handkerchief and managed a weak smile.

"There," she said to the stunned policeman, "you can have it."

Still feeling sick, the two women crawled back on the train for the ride to the downtown train station. There would be no milk tonight for their little girls, but nobody else would drink it either.

My mother had heard these stories many times. The music stopped again. There was another announcement to stand by. Despite the warm September morning, my mother shivered. More than one hour had passed since the first announcement. Finally, Hitler's voice came over the air waves. German troops had occupied the Free City of Danzig and shots had been exchanged in Poland. The Polish Corridor would be German again. A madman was trying to conquer the world. World War II had started.

On the same morning, long before the Fuehrer spoke, my grandparents and I boarded a train in the Stuttgart train station. Still a little sleepy, I looked up at the wooden roof covering the platforms. Rays of early morning sun found their way between the tracks, making them look like silvery roads.

I loved the train station. My grandpa, a railroad man,

worked there. Sometimes he took me to the top of the big tower. I could see trains coming and leaving the station continuously. Grandpa knew where every train came from or where it was going. He told me of faraway places like Paris, Madrid, Rome and Warsaw. Some trains even went to Turkey, and some had names. There was the *Dalmatian Express* from Rijeka on the Adriatic Sea on its way to Ostende in Belgium. The *Tauern Express* came from Belgrade and also went to Belgium. The *Austria Express* came from Vienna and went to Holland.

I never tired of watching the trains come slowly out of the station, and after just a short time, disappear into the tunnel between Stuttgart and Cannstatt. The trains coming from the faraway places shot out from the tunnel, then slowed and somehow, in the maze of tracks, found the right one to bring them into the station.

I was excited. I had ridden trains before, but this time I would be on a train taking me to places I had never seen before, places Grandpa had told me about. Every year Grandpa got a free family rail pass, and this year it was used for a three-day vacation.

After about one hour, the train stopped to take on new passengers. An elderly man and woman took seats across from us. The woman, obviously shaken, asked if we had heard the news. Hitler had declared war. She and her husband had heard it on the radio that morning. She was afraid that their son would be drafted.

"Do you think if there really is a war, this will happen?" the woman asked.

"Yes," my grandmother replied. "When war was declared in 1914, my husband was drafted immediately."

The couple got off at the next station. I did not understand what the adults talked about, but soon the somber mood changed again. My grandparents said this vacation should be a happy one, and it would be.

The train, its steam engine whistling, entered the Black Forest with its breathtaking scenery. We passed the city of Freiburg and entered a narrow valley called the Hoellental Valley. Natural rock walls rose high up into the sky on both sides of the valley.

"Look up," Grandpa said.

High above us were two rocks, one on each side of the narrow valley. This was the "deer jump." Legend told that long ago a hunter followed a deer through the forest, only to lose him when the deer jumped across the gorge from one rock to another.

Late in the afternoon, we reached Lindau on Lake Constance and spent the night there in a hotel. Then, early the next morning, we boarded a ferry for the crossing to Romanshorn in Switzerland. I was looking forward to see Switzerland, my first visit to another country. However, when the ship arrived in the Romanshorn harbor, Swiss officials refused to let us tie up at the dock. They claimed their country was a neutral country that had to close its borders to a country that was now at war.

Some passengers became very angry and said, "Well, if they won't let us set foot on their land, we are close enough to spit on them." Leaning over the railing, many of them did.

The ship had to return to the German shore. The next day we boarded a train again for the return trip to Stuttgart. This time we took a different route. After a few hours, we stopped at a large train station. There was a delay, the conductor told us.

Our train was diverted to a side track to make room for a long train waiting for soldiers to board. Their wives, children, sweethearts, sisters, fathers, mothers, friends and neighbors had come to see them off. They carried bouquets of late summer flowers and gave them to the soldiers. Someone fastened a huge wreath of flowers to the front of the train.

The soldiers, happy and laughing, leaned out the windows and yelled, "We will be home by Christmas. It will be all over by then. We will have whipped them!"

Finally, the steam whistle sounded. The soldiers waved their bouquets.

"*Auf Wiedersehen*," they called, "we will be back soon!"

Weeping women reached up to clutch outstretched hands. Some ran alongside the slow-moving train for a couple of minutes; others waved their handkerchiefs in final farewell until the train disappeared around a curve. For many, it was the last time they saw their men.

The war was not over by Christmas, nor by the next Christmas or the next. When it finally ended five years and eight months later, many of the young men who had left with flowers in their arms had died and were buried in foreign soil in unmarked graves. Of those who survived, many found that their families had been killed by bombs that rained from heaven, had starved to death or had just disappeared.

I was nine years old when the war started and fifteen when it ended. The years in between are permanently engraved on the souls of those who experienced them. As more and more men were drafted "to do their duty for the fatherland," more and more women took over their duties at home. They worked in factories, drove streetcars, carried the mail and loaded freight trains. Huge billboards screamed their messages to the German people, messages like "One People, One Country, One Leader", "Today Germany, Tomorrow the World", "Total War", "Careful, Enemy is Listening" and many others.

The beginning of the war brought immediate rationing for food and household goods. At first the restrictions were bearable. Potatoes, vegetables and fruits were not immediately rationed. Most German housewives had a stock of basic food and home-canned food in their larders. As months and then years went by, the situation worsened. Food rations became smaller. Housewives had to invent ways to stretch meager supplies. Soup kitchens opened to feed people after bombings, and people managed to survive. The real famine started after the war in 1945.

My father was drafted into the army in 1941 at the age of thirty-four. Every able-bodied adult still at home, male and female, had to work to receive ration cards. My mother was drafted to work on the assembly line in an ammunition factory. She hated it, but she was afraid to voice her opinion about Hitler to the other girls, who all seemed, or at least pretended to be, in awe of the Fuehrer. She came home every night complaining about the bad air in the building. None of the other girls would let her open a window.

Then one day, my mother and a girlfriend decided to join a group who entertained wounded soldiers in hospitals. Here, she could use her musical talent by singing and playing the piano. She and her friend were soon sent to entertain soldiers in the field. She loved it and was traveling for weeks at a time.

I now spent more and more time with my grandparents. Grandpa's employment with the railroad entitled him to a garden spot, a small plot of land at the edge of the city, for which he paid a few marks rent each month. Many other railroad families had garden plots there too.

Grandfather built a tiny arbor-like garden house and put an old metal roof on it. Grandmother put an old rusty tub under the edge of the roof to catch rainwater for watering the plants. Every inch of ground was planted with lettuce, radishes, leek, a few potatoes, cucumbers, onions, carrots, kohlrabi, spinach and mangold, a spinach-like green vegetable. There were a few heads of cabbage, two or three tomato plants, and even a few strawberry and rhubarb plants. As soon as one vegetable was harvested, another one was planted in its space.

Clinging to the very edge of the plot was a gooseberry bush, one black and one red currant bush and a few hills of chives. When cut into small pieces, chives were used to make a watery, meatless cabbage and potato soup look elegant and taste good. As a small luxury, Grandma planted a few dahlia bulbs and several asters.

Grandpa always turned the ground for planting with a spade, but Grandma and I planted and took care of the garden. Grandma was raised in the country and knew how to raise a garden, but she was worried about fertilizing the plants to make them grow. One day, much to the consternation and absolute horror of my mother, Grandma found a solution.

Gasoline was rationed and in very short supply. Because of the rationing, horse drawn wagons were seen in the streets again. Grandmother, armed with an old dustpan and bucket, posted herself in front of the house. As soon as she saw a horse-drawn vehicle approach, she resolutely grabbed her dustpan and bucket and followed them down the middle of the street, hoping the horses would drop something. When they did, she would triumphantly scoop it up and drop it in the bucket.

My mother declared that either she or Grandma would not be part of our family anymore, and she always prayed that none of her friends would witness this spectacle. She was aghast when other women followed

Grandma's example.

The gardens were fertilized and the streets kept clean. It was a fifteen-minute walk from Grandma's house to the garden. Grandma walked briskly carrying her bucket full of treasure, defying anyone to say something about the aroma rising from it. I skipped along, carrying a basket to bring back vegetables or berries. Once at the garden, I could play with other children and trade some of our harvest with them. A few fortunate families had a plot with a peach or apple tree. One childless couple had a cherry tree. They were always very generous and shared their cherries with us.

The garden has remained one of my good war memories. For a while, it was a good place to visit. Eventually though, the air raids became more numerous. Some of my garden friends did not come any more. Many had lost their homes and moved away to find shelter with relatives or friends in other towns. Some of my friends had been killed by bombs and fire. A few had no other place to go and moved into their tiny garden houses. One night bombs fell on the gardens, splintering the tiny houses, killing their inhabitants, shredding trees, leaving huge craters where plants had grown, taking away even this meager supply of food and the simple joy the place had given us in the midst of upheaval.

THE FIRST AIR RAID WARNING

Hermann Goering, the field marshal of the Air Force, promised that no enemy airplane would be able to cross German borders. It would be automatically shot down. If even one enemy plane penetrated German territory, he would change his name to Mayer (a very common German surname). Some people were skeptical. Why was a complete blackout ordered shortly after the war began, if there was no danger? My friends and I heard the promise from our teachers. We believed them, and we felt safe.

It happened anyway. Early one Sunday morning, air raid sirens sounded, waking up the sleeping city. It was June 30, 1940. I spent the weekend with my grandparents in the western part of town. Oma, my grandmother, drowsily groped for her flashlight and shone it on the alarm clock on her night stand. The time was 1:15 a.m. The sirens still howled. Opa, my grandfather, had already jumped out of bed.

"This is an air raid," he yelled. "Take the child and go to the cellar. I have to warn the others!"

I hated it when he called me "the child." After all, I was ten years old, going on eleven.

At first, Oma thought this alarm was a practice one. There had been some in the past. But at this time of night? No, that could not be possible. Opa pulled on his heavy boots and ran out the door and down the stairs, clad only in his union suit, untied shoelaces flying. He raced up and down the stairs, waving his flashlight, knocking on every door, yelling, "Hurry, go to the cellar, go to the cellar, this is an air raid!"

Apartment doors opened. People crowded into the stairwell, shock on their faces. Women in long nightgowns, their hair in disarray, carried small children. Most of their husbands already served in the German army. My grandfather was one of the few men still left in the apartment building. He was too old to be drafted, and he worked for the railroad.

Utter chaos prevailed. People rushed down to the cellar, then rushed back up again to save some treasured item. Opa still yelled instructions that nobody paid attention to. In our apartment, Oma slipped into a robe, put a blanket around my shoulder and grabbed one of Opa's railroad coats. We went down the stairs as fast as we could. We encountered Opa on the second landing, still running around in a flap. Oma managed to throw the coat over his shoulders. Usually, my grandfather was a calm and organized man who never lost his composure.

By now, the stairwell was crowded with panic-stricken people. One woman was crying. During the commotion, her cat had slipped outside. The air raid warden, who had just arrived, forbade her to go outside. Another woman raced back upstairs to fetch Hansele, her canary. We children all knew and loved Hansele, and of course he must be saved.

Two elderly sisters, old maids, emerged from their apartment. They were completely dressed. Each carried a small suitcase and a large handbag. Black hats, adorned with red felt flowers, sat slightly askew on top of their silken night caps. They sent shocked glances in my grandpa's direction.

"This must be the highlight of their lives, seeing a man in his underwear," giggled one woman.

Forty-five minutes later, at 2:00 a.m., the all-clear sounded. British planes had flown over our city but dropped their deadly cargo on another town. No bombs had fallen on Stuttgart, not this time at least. However, this would change soon.

As we slowly went back upstairs to our apartment, I heard the woman who carried Hansele in his cage say to the bird, "Hansele, now we can call Hermann Goering Mr. Mayer; don't you agree?"

Her neighbor bent down to her and whispered,

"True, but you can only talk to your Hansele about it, to nobody else."

All families living in the apartment house, as well as those living in neighboring houses, were called for a meeting the next morning. It was decided to furnish the cellars with cots, tables and chairs. Sandbags were piled high around the walls and buckets were filled with water to fight fires. Each family was assigned a space to keep a few belongings. Tunnels would be dug under the houses from cellar to cellar for escape routes, should one or several houses be bombed, catch fire or collapse. This was a wise decision and saved many lives later.

The construction of the tunnels was done by the older women with the help of the children. The younger women were working in industries important for the war, as were the few men who were still at home. The work started immediately. The women dug out the dirt with shovels and spades, and the children carried it out in buckets and dumped it in the back yard. After a few days of digging, several soldiers arrived. They stabilized and framed the walls, then installed steel fire doors between the cellars of each house.

The blackout was now even more strictly enforced. There were no streetlights, no lights in store windows or on advertising boards after dark. Street curbs, corners of houses, outside steps, fences and even tree trunks were painted white to help people find their way in the dark. Everyone wore phosphorescent pins and brooches so that they would not collide with each other on dark nights. Cars drove with covered headlights, emitting only a small ray of light through small slits in their covers. Trains and streetcars had their lights dimmed as low as possible, and people prayed for moonless nights.

Bunkers and air raid shelters were built around the city. People who helped physically construct these shelters had priority to use them during air raids. They were issued passes to gain entry and usually assigned seats. When the shelters were full, the doors were locked. Public shelters were open to the public as long as there was room for everyone.

My grandfather had inherited a small house and orchard in the country from his Aunt Karoline. We spent most of our vacations there, and I loved the place. After the first air raid warning, my grandparents decided to move a few belongings such as paintings, books and china to their little country house.

"Just in case something might happen," they would say. The decision was prudent, because these were the only things that survived the war.

Elfriede E. Wilde

Der Inhaber dieser Karte ist in den

Bahnhofbunker Untertürkheim

eingeteilt.

Rückseite beachten

Werkluftschutzleiter:

Frau Else Seiler

Diese Karte ist stets bei sich zu führen und beim Betreten des Schutzraumes dem Ordner vorzuzeigen. Wer ohne Ausweis den Schutzraum betreten will wird abgewiesen.

Nicht übertragbar

Bei Versetzung oder Austritt ist diese Karte an den Abteilungsleiter zurückzugeben.

Pass for Train Station Bunker
Stuttgart-Untertuerkheim

AUNT KAROLINE'S HOUSE

Red tile roof, glinting in the evening sun
Shiny windows framed by green shutters
The scent of vanilla and raspberries wafting through the rooms

Entrance hall draped in rusty-red Hessian cloth
High-backed chairs in the parlor, covered with worn red velvet
A matching red sofa, suffocating under a sea of pillows
Aunt Karoline in the kitchen, waving a wooden spoon
Reigning over kitchen chaos
Mounds of luscious, plump raspberries
Sweet as new wine
Picked early in the morning
When the sun claimed the right to a new day

Turned into ruby red jellies, melt-in-your-mouth cakes
Wine-red juices, and raspberry brandy

We found a bottle of it one day
My friends and I
It burned our throats with a fiery fury
But left a lingering sweetness

Wild roses, picked at the edge of the woods
Glow in an elegant gilded vase on the red tablecloth
More beautiful than bouquets brought by a lover
An eternity ago, she tells us, as she graciously accepts our gift

We sit in the high-backed chairs

Elfriede E. Wilde

Trying to keep our backs straight
Like the ladies who come on Sunday afternoons
Dressed in ridiculous bright colors
Wearing hats as big as wagon wheels
Gossiping words flowing smoothly
From lips crowned with mustaches

Aunt Karoline dabs vanilla behind her ears
Real vanilla, not the imitation
We sip raspberry juice from crystal goblets
Daintily pick up tiny pieces of cake between our fingers
And feel important
And wonder what happened to the mysterious lover

One day, after Aunt Karoline was put to rest
Under blankets of red roses
People came, rich as Croesus
And tore down the house and garden

Where children drank from crystal goblets
And raspberries grew in an enchanted garden
They built a cement palace
Ugly like Hades' dwelling

But the faint fragrance of vanilla and raspberry
still lingers in the air.

THE TRAIN

I do not think we should have gone to the train station on that cold, cloudy day. Since my grandpa worked for the railroad, he had access to some areas where others could not go. We walked out of the train station towards the north station. Grandpa wore his railroad uniform, showing his right to be there. For some strange reason, I still remember the coat I wore. It was a gray wool coat, my favorite coat in all my life, and I was proud of my stylish gray beret.

I do not know why Grandpa took me with him on that day. He often took me to the train station. Sometimes, we climbed up into the tower, and he showed me all the trains coming in from strange places like Hungary, Spain, France, Holland and others. So, it was not unusual that I accompanied him on this day also.

Soon I saw people crowded closely together, standing in front of a freight train. Several freight cars were hitched to a black steam engine that was hissing and belching smoke. There were a few single men, but I could tell that most were families.

Everybody wore heavy coats on this cold day. The men wore black hats, and some women also wore dark hats. I do not remember seeing any bright colors. The only bright color was the yellow Star of David that all of them wore on the upper left side of their coats, the word *Jude* (Jew) written inside the star. Only very young children did not wear a star.

The people carried small suitcases. Some of the men carried leather briefcases. The children clung to their parents. I could tell they were scared. The SS soldiers, carrying guns and holding large German shepherds on leashes, encircled the crowd.

Our teachers told us that all Jews were evil people. If we saw one in the street, we should not speak to them. They were not "pure" Germans, even if their families had lived here for generations. Some houses had the word *Jude* written on the outside walls, showing that Jews lived there. We were not allowed to go into Jewish stores anymore.

Hitler wrote, "There is only one sacred human right, and this right at the same time is the most holy obligation, namely: to make sure that the blood will be kept pure, that through protecting the best of mankind a noble development of these humans will be made possible."

Of course, we were taught that we were the best of mankind, superior to anyone else in the world. We were Aryans!

Grandpa and I stood across from the train track behind the corner of a building, watching. Nobody saw us. The crowd was very quiet. Even the little children were quiet. We could not understand what the soldiers with guns were saying, but they must have been calling names, because one by one people came forward and climbed onto the train. Some turned around in the doorway and looked back. If they lingered too long, they were prodded with a gun to move.

Grandpa looked like he was searching for a familiar face. Maybe he was looking for his good friend Mr. Schaefer who could sing so beautifully that everyone said he should have been an opera star. He and Grandpa belonged to an Esperanto group long before Hitler became the leader of Germany. Esperanto is an international language invented by Dr.

L. Zamenhof, a Jew.

Grandpa and Mr. Schaefer loved speaking with people from different countries in a language everyone understood. They were sure it was the language of the future. Grandpa promised he would teach me this language when I started school in 1936. But that was the year when Hitler forbade Esperanto groups and the language itself. I never heard Grandpa nor Mr. Schaefer utter one word in this language again.

Mr. Schaefer was a Jehovah's Witness. He refused to raise his arm in the required Hitler greeting and say "Heil Hitler" (Hail Hitler). It had become the public greeting for everyone. It was used to enter an official office; students greeted teachers in the mornings with these words; and friends greeted each other with "Heil Hitler" when meeting in the street.

Mr. Schaefer said he would only raise his arm to hail the Lord. Grandpa begged him to say the greeting. Grandpa said that it did not mean a thing. Mr. Schaefer was warned several times, but he always refused to comply. One day he, his wife and his children disappeared. Others disappeared too, not only Jews. Was Grandpa looking for his friend now? My mother and my grandparents had Jewish friends, but we did not visit them anymore. I could not see Mr. Schaefer or any of his family in the crowd; so I thought they were safe. They were not. We left before the train did.

"Where are these people going?" I asked Grandpa.

"I have been told they are going to a nice place where they can work," he replied.

Our teachers told us the same thing. Much later, I heard that Jews had to report on certain days at a certain time to an assigned place, with little luggage. From there, they were taken to the train station, usually to a track outside the main station. Rumors circulated where the Jews were taken, but nobody knew anything for certain. People feared talking about it. Only many years later did we hear about the Holocaust, the concentration camps, the murder of six million Jews by Hitler.

Irmgard was one of my mother's friends with whom she grew up. Irmgard was Jewish. They went to school together long before Hitler became Chancellor of Germany. My mother married, and the two friends drifted apart. After Irmgard had to wear the yellow Star of David on her clothing, my mother became afraid to associate with her.

My grandmother was not afraid. She continued to pray for them, hoping they would take the chance to leave their business and emigrate. However, the family stayed in town. All association with Jewish families was forbidden. Even though the families did not visit anymore, Grandma still greeted them when they passed in the street, which was a most dangerous undertaking. Had someone reported it, Grandma would have been in terrible trouble, maybe even arrested. Then came Crystal Night on November 9, 1938, when the synagogues were burned. Irmgard and her mother died that night. After her father had been taken away, she and her mother hung themselves in their store.

EDUCATION AND PHYSICAL FITNESS

Hitler planned to create a master race to conquer the world. He needed educated and healthy people to accomplish this. Education and sports were very important under Hitler's regime.

In 1943, at age thirteen, I took a four-day pre-college entrance examination and passed. By fall, I was in a camp in the Swabian Alb. We were a group of about thirty girls with three female teachers called "leaders" who prepared us for college entry in spring. Besides our regular classes each day, we had to take care of everything else, cooking, cleaning and doing laundry. We lived a Spartan life.

Discipline was strictly enforced every hour of the day. Even our free time was scheduled. I realized much later that this actually prepared me to handle difficulties I encountered later in my life.

Winter came early with harsh temperatures. I shared a room with two other girls. We slept in unheated rooms on straw mattresses covered with heavy featherbeds that we had brought from home. Every morning at 5:00 a.m., the morning whistle woke us up. We pulled on our jogging suits, lined up in the court yard, then jogged for about fifteen minutes, even if the snow was knee deep. As soon as we came back to the barracks, we sponged ourselves down with cold water from top to toe. Surprisingly, we never got sick.

Then, we prepared our rooms for inspection. The hardest thing for me was to fix the straw mattresses with sharp corners. During the first few weeks at camp, my mattress did not often pass inspection. It was pulled out of my bed and thrown on the floor by one of the teachers, and I had to do it over. On weekends, the lockers were inspected. Every item had to be folded by metric measurement. If this was not accurate, all our possessions were thrown on the floor, and we had to correct it. We all helped each other adjust, doing chores and studying.

The teachers promised that we could go home for a week for Christmas vacation. Due to increased bombings of Stuttgart, the vacation was cancelled. Having no mail delivery for days before the holidays did not help improve our spirits. We did not know that our mail was held on purpose and that we would receive it on Christmas Eve as special gifts.

Finally, on Christmas Eve, we were called to the dining room. A table was loaded with letters and packages from our families. My mother's gift was a copy of *Gudrun's Death* by Gerhard Schumann. She stood in line for hours at a bookstore to purchase the book. It was printed on paper that soon turned yellow. I carried the book in my survival bag during air raids, and I still treasure it today. Grandmother sent a box of apples from her garden that I shared with everyone.

After supper Els, the head leader of the camp, told us to change into our jogging suits, put on our heaviest coats and line up in formation in front of the building. It was a freezing but starlit night. We were shivering and grumbling under our breath. We could not believe that we were forced on a march on Christmas Eve.

After about fifteen minutes, we reached the edge of the woods and continued on a small foot path. Suddenly, we saw lights shimmering through the trees. A clearing opened in front of us and in the middle of the clearing stood the tallest Christmas tree I had ever seen, decorated with live candles. We stood in awe, speechless for a minute or two. Forgotten was the march in the freezing cold.

We formed a circle around the tree, held hands, and sang Christmas carols. We must have sung for about twenty minutes before marching back to camp.

Only later did I realize that some of our songs were old Christian Christmas hymns, a rarity for young people at that time. It was the most memorable Christmas Eve in my entire life.

Since blackouts were strictly enforced, our teachers took a great risk to arrange this special evening for us. If their superiors had found out, they would have been in deep trouble. Several young farmers who lived in the small town, offered to put the candles on the tree and light them. Everyone prayed that no enemy airplanes would fly over that night. The lights on the tree would have been visible to them.

One day, my mother told me in one of her letters how thankful she was that I lived in a remote place that probably was not a target for bombing by enemy airplanes. At this time, she lived in our apartment in Ulm. One night, bombs fell in what seemed only seconds after the sirens sounded their warning. She rushed out of the house with only her purse slung over her shoulder. Anxious to reach a nearby bomb shelter, she and others took a shortcut across a meadow instead of using the street.

A bomb exploded close by. A soldier who ran behind her yelled at her to get down. Seconds before the next bomb exploded, he pushed her to the ground, then threw himself on top of her, shielding her from it. A few minutes later, everything grew still. The planes had left.

My mother told the man she thought it was safe now to get up. He did not move. She struggled to get out from under him and was finally able to push him a little to the side. People came to help her. The soldier who had saved her life was dead. She did not even know what he looked like.

In spring of 1944, we transferred to the teachers' college in Esslingen, now called LBA (Lehrerbildungsanstalt). We joined other students, but our group stayed close together. We felt superior. We slept in large dormitories. There was no cooking now, no laundry or cleaning, but lots of studying.

Our most important subject was physical education, followed by history and biology. I hated biology, not the subject, but the biology teacher who continuously smoked a pipe with foul-smelling tobacco. Since cigarettes and tobacco were rationed, we wondered what kind of weeds he was smoking.

My favorite subjects were German, history and literature. History included mythology, which fascinated me. I felt that I really was a child of the Gods and that they would protect me.

We had a large library at home, and I was raised in a reading family. My grandfather taught me to read when I was four years old. He may not have realized that he gave me a gift for life. Unfortunately, most of our books were lost in the war.

I also loved sports. A good long-distance swimmer already, I trained in broad jump and won some competitions. I am in my late eighties now and still swim ten to twelve laps nearly every day in an Olympic-size pool.

NIGHT OF HORROR

The night of September 12, 1944, is burned into my soul forever. We were granted a few days of fall vacation. I was looking forward to spending some time in the country with my grandmother, away from strict teachers ruling my life and accounting for every minute of the day. Grandma was getting their little country house ready for winter, and I was going to help her.

Our classes dismissed in the afternoon. I walked to the train station with several of my friends, and we happily boarded the train for the short twenty-minute ride to Stuttgart. When we arrived at the station, even though there was damage from previous bombings, we found it teeming with soldiers, Red Cross workers, passengers and refugees who had arrived from the Eastern part of the country. Our goodbyes were short; we would see each other again in just a few days.

Due to the bombings, streetcars often were not running on schedules and sometimes not running at all. So, I walked to my grandparents' apartment in the western part of the city. I would spend the night there, then meet Grandpa the next morning after he got off from work and accompany him on our trip to the country.

Many homes, historical buildings and churches had either been destroyed or heavily damaged by many bombings. But this place was where I grew up and where Grandpa had taught me the history of the city since I was a little girl. My heart was heavy to see so much destruction, but it was still my home, the town I would always love.

The air raid sirens woke me up before midnight. I grabbed my already-packed little suitcase and my shoulder bag and rushed down to the cellar. Unlike the chaos during the first air raid warning in June 1940, people were now prepared. Most everyone slept completely dressed to reach a shelter in minutes. Since the bombings had increased, some people even slept on cots in the cellars.

The residents of the house assembled quickly in the old wine cellar deep below the basement. It seemed only minutes until we heard the first bombs fall. The walls and the floor shook, dust crumbled from the ceiling. The only light came from a few flickering candles and a couple of flashlights.

We covered our mouths and noses with handkerchiefs. Prayer had become rare in Germany, especially for young people, but someone started to pray. If my grandma had been here, she would have prayed too. By now, there was a constant rumble of falling bombs. We expected the ceiling to come down on us any second, or the floor to split open and swallow us. Someone suggested that we try to go outside before we were all crushed to death. Not everyone wanted to leave; they still felt safer in the cellar.

I decided to go with the group that wanted to leave. Leaving everything behind but my shoulder bag with my ID papers, some money and a few other small items, I carefully followed the others up to the basement, then to the first floor. The front door and part of the wall next to it was torn away. When we stepped out into the street, there was a blazing inferno, fire and smoke all around us. Even the air seemed on fire. I was sure the end of the world had come, and we were plunging directly into Hell. I found out later that we actually stood at the edge of the fire–one block further in and we probably would not have survived.

Somehow, I found two of my girlfriends in the burning street. In the chaos, both were separated from their families. We decided to stay together and try to make our way to the Schlossplatz, the Castle Square, where we hoped we would be safe. Climbing over mountains of rubble and around dead bodies, we made our way from house to house, from street to street. A burning building collapsed behind us just seconds after we passed it. It seemed impossible to find our way between burning buildings, but we made it. The real heroes that night were the firemen who managed to keep small passages open by spraying them with water, enabling people to flee.

We finally reached the Schlossplatz. Wounded, dying and dead people lay on the grass. I remember an old woman lifting up her worn, scorched dress and tearing strips from her equally worn petticoat to tie around her husband's bleeding head. I was sure that he was already dead.

A gray morning dawned. No sunlight shone all day. I am not sure if the day was just cloudy or if the sun could not penetrate the smoke. I could not see even one flower in the once beautiful gardens.

The smoke made it hard to breathe; so we decided to go to the fountain at the edge of the square to dip our handkerchiefs in the water, then hold it over our mouths and noses to help us breathe. The basin was a cauldron of blood. People had used their clothing or whatever rags they could find to wash the wounds of their loved ones. They had dipped and wrung out blood-soaked cloths in the basin of the fountain again and again in desperate attempts to keep their loved ones alive, mingling the blood of many with the water. I learned later that the heat from the fire was so strong that the damaged chestnut trees started to bud and bloom again from heat shock, even though it was fall.

I am still not able to completely describe the scenes of that night—the firestorm, the dead, people running, screaming, falling. Other air raids happened before and after this day. But for me, this raid is the one burned into my soul forever. Thirty-three years later, during one of my visits in Stuttgart, I was finally able to go to the well again. Fifty-six years later, at the urging of my husband, I wrote a poem about it.

The "Blood" Well
Stuttgart 1977

STUTTGART, SEPTEMBER 1944

Fire raining from the sky
engulfing the earth
flames driven by a roaring storm

The stench of burning flesh and bones
mingles with acrid smoke from burning cloth, wood, trees, steel
and blood-soaked stones.

Houses burst apart,
throwing sparks, like fireworks, high into the red night.

People running, screaming, falling, some never getting up,
 mired in burning asphalt roads.

A woman's clothes on fire,
a child's hair ablaze.

Terror, no water, no place to hide,
I can't breathe, my eyes sting, my shoes are scorched.
skin peels off the soles of my feet

My world, in flames around me, disappears forever.

    During that night, 957 people were killed, 1,600 injured and 50,000 people lost their homes, their belongings, and they had nowhere to go (Bardua, 144.) In comparison to other cities, Stuttgart fared much better. Hamburg, Pforzheim, Dresden and other cities lost many more lives. Due to Stuttgart's location in the Neckar Valley, bomb shelters were dug into the surrounding hills. Many of the older houses had deep wine cellars that sheltered people, thus many lives were spared. But even with these shelters, death was busy during the night of September 12, 1944.

MY MOTHER'S DREAMS

During school vacations or on weekend visits at home, I remember my mother sitting up at night when the electricity was shut off, flashlight shining on pages, reading cookbooks like story books. One night while sitting in the cellar during an air raid warning, she made a list of menus she wanted to cook after the war. They were simple dishes—cabbage and mashed potatoes, fish with boiled potatoes, pancakes with applesauce, spinach with fried eggs, vanilla pudding made with real milk and bread dumplings. I found her handwritten menu list in one of her cookbooks after she died.

One of her big dreams was to buy pretzels and dunk them in milk with lots of sugar added. It was the first food she planned to buy as soon as the war was over. However, it took years after the war until she could do this or cook all her dreamed-of menus.

Her dreams also included wearing elegant dresses again, and shoes without holes in the sole, having a little heat in winter and never, never being hungry again. Dreaming like this was her way to survive.

THE LAST DAYS OF THE WAR

Some of the girls in my college class were far from home. Due to the bombings and slow mail service, they heard little from their families. Most of them had fathers or brothers in the war, and they did not know what had happened to them. Now there was fear. An unknown enemy had crossed the Rhine, the Neckar, and was coming closer every day. Rumors flew, frightening rumors that all girls would be raped by the invading soldiers, the boys would be tortured and killed, the teachers arrested and deported to places unknown.

Early on the morning of April 16, 1945, a frightened group of girls assembled for English class. The teacher collected yesterday's homework, then started to write something on the blackboard. Nobody paid much attention. The door opened and the Dean of Women hurried in. Her clothes were rumpled, she looked exhausted, like she had been up all night.

"Girls," she said, "we have decided to dismiss school for a short vacation. Try to get to your homes. This will be over soon. We will be back here in a week or two to continue our studies. Take only a few things. Everything will still be here when you come back. You are dismissed right now." She raised her hand, "Heil Hitler," turned on her heel and left the room.

Everyone sat stunned for a few moments. The teacher carefully erased the blackboard. She too looked tired and worn out, like she had been up all night.

"How shall we get home?" one of the girls asked. "We heard yesterday that the trains stopped running."

"I don't know," the teacher said, "but you must leave right now."

We filed out of the room in an orderly manner just as we had been taught. Once outside, we raced for our rooms. Erika, my roommate, was already there, throwing things into a suitcase.

"Elisabeth, did you hear that they arrested Professor Schneider last night because he said the war was lost, and the people who still listened to Hitler were fools?"

Professor Schneider taught literature, my favorite subject, and he was my favorite teacher. He never could remember my name, nor anyone else's. He always called me the girl with the Titian red hair.

Without further explanation Erika hugged me, and yelled "I will see you in a week or two." She rushed out the door, dragging her heavy suitcase behind her.

I threw my English book on my bed, then took a small bag from my closet. In it, I put my only good sweater, my best underwear, the one without holes, a pair of socks and my well-worn tennis shoes. I grabbed my toothbrush, comb, hairbrush, all well-used, and my last sliver of soap and threw them in the bag. From underneath the straw mattress on my bed, I pulled the small stash of dried bread I had saved from our meager bread rations. I hid it carefully at the bottom of the bag. At the last minute, I took my English book and stuck it into the bag.

"This is ridiculous" I mumbled, "what am I going to do with an English book on vacation?"

I took the book out of the bag and threw it on my bed, then went to the small bookcase and reached for my science book. Science was not my favorite subject, but I would concentrate on studying it during the vacation. The door burst open. Ruth and Elsa, two of my friends, rushed in.

"Come on, Elisabeth," they yelled, "let's go."

I looked at the book in my hand, threw it on the bed

and picked up the English book again. I put it on top of my few belongings and shut the bag. Then I grabbed my coat, made from one of my grandmother's old pre-war coats, and followed my friends out the door.

The scene in the hall was pandemonium. Students and teachers were running everywhere. Our music teacher, a young, pretty woman, rushed past us, stopped and turned back. She looked at us with worried eyes.

"You are not living here in the city, are you?" she asked. We shook our heads. "I am praying that you can make your way home. May God be with you."

"What a strange thing to say," I thought. What did God have to do with this chaos and man-made madness?

My friends and I lived in different towns to the east and northeast. We planned to stay together at least part of the way. We rushed down the stairs and out into the courtyard, following other students. Some were in a state of panic. Those who lived west of the city were afraid to leave. Many of them were crying, but nobody cared.

Rumors were flying. Someone said that Stuttgart was already taken by enemy soldiers who were looting, raping and destroying what little was left in the already nearly destroyed city. We heard gunfire in the distance. Were the sounds from German weapons that would protect us, or was the enemy this close already? We headed for the highway leading toward Stuttgart, discarding rumors that the city was already occupied by enemy soldiers. We had to reach the outskirts of the city, then go east.

We were stunned by what we saw. The road was jammed with thousands of refugees. Teams of oxen pulled wagons, loaded with women, children and household goods. Others pulled small hand carts or pushed baby buggies. But most were on foot carrying children, suitcases, knapsacks or cardboard boxes. A few lucky ones had bicycles.

Ruth, Elsa and I, unencumbered by heavy luggage, pushed our way through the crowd. To our left was the town, one of the few that had escaped heavy bombings. To our right stretched a mountain ridge. Bomb shelters were cut deep into its bowels. We had spent many nights in the mountain, seeking shelter from falling bombs. For a moment, we pondered if we would be safer in the mountain than on the highway. Army vehicles, their shrill horns demanding the right of way, traveled in both directions.

About an hour after we left our school, we slowed down. The crowd had thinned out, the bulk of the people lumbering behind us, carrying their heavy burdens. We jumped at the sound of a car horn. A Mercedes convertible, probably confiscated from some formerly wealthy German, pulled up next to us. An officer and his driver sat in the front seats. The back seat was stacked high with boxes, clearly labeled *ammunition*.

"*Guten Tag*, girls," the dashing young officer called, "do you want a ride?"

"There is no room in your car," Ruth said, pointing to the ammunition boxes.

"Well, it is a nice sunny day. You can sit on top of the boxes," the officer replied.

Such an offer would have been inconceivable even a few months ago. Now all we wanted was to get home as fast as possible, to feel the safety of our families around us. Ignoring the unfriendly stares and provocative remarks of some older women nearby, we climbed atop the boxes, clutching our bags tightly to our chests. The officer grinned, then smartly doffed his hat to the women and waved, omitting the usual "Heil Hitler" salute. The car sped away. We clung to the boxes to keep from falling off.

Soon the highway became crowded again. People

from smaller towns and villages along the Neckar River joined the refugees. The Mercedes dodged farm wagons, baby carriages, handcarts and people. When we arrived at the Neckar Bridge in Bad Cannstatt, a suburb of Stuttgart, we got out. The car continued to the heart of the city.

The gunfire was closer now. My friends and I joined the crowd rushing across the bridge. On the other side, people fought for space on several trucks about to take off. They tried to put suitcases, cardboard boxes, bedding, bags and baby carriages on the trucks, items which were promptly removed by soldiers.

"No heavy luggage," one soldier shouted.

Ruth, Elsa and I clutched our small bags and jumped on the back of a truck already near capacity. Two soldiers and two very old men with armbands identifying them as home militia, squeezed in behind us.

One soldier called to the driver, "Let's get out of here!"

The motor roared, and the truck took off at high speed, leaving behind frantic people who tried to cling to the sideboards. Only seconds later, the air raid sirens sounded their warning.

Since enemy airfields were so close now, no advanced warning could be given anymore. The sirens wailed with a rapidly changing up and down tone. This tone was an "acute alarm," meaning that people should take cover immediately. Bombs usually fell within minutes or even seconds after the warning.

Everyone on the truck braced themselves for a sudden stop. Women clutched children to their bodies, preparing to jump off and find shelter in ditches or ruins of destroyed buildings. The stop did not come. Instead, the truck gathered speed and raced out of town. It was clear the driver hoped to reach the safety of the sparsely populated countryside.

Soon we came to an intersection. A truck coming from another direction was trying to escape the city too. They both reached the intersection at the same time. Metal crashed into metal with a horrible sound. I was thrown into the air. My head hit an iron bar supporting the tarp. People screamed. Several were thrown out of the truck. One of the old men flew through the air. He hit the ground, head first, and lay still.

I felt something hot and sticky in my hair, running down the side of my face. The collar of my blouse turned red. Surprisingly, I still clutched my bag. Where were Elsa and Ruth? I felt dizzy and clung to the truck's sideboard. Then I saw them. They had been thrown out of the truck and sat on the ground, stunned, but apparently unhurt.

A young redheaded woman who stood next to me unwound a scarf from her neck and gently wrapped it around my head.

"Come on," she said, "we have to get out of here."

With her help, I climbed out of the truck. A soldier, a sleeve torn from his uniform and blood seeping down his arm, walked up to us.

"There is a first aid station down the road about a block from here," he said. "Can you get the girl there?"

"I will take her," the young woman said.

Elsa and Ruth, their clothes torn, rushed over. Ruth started to cry when she saw the blood-soaked scarf around my head.

"We have to get help for you," she said, "but where?"

Mangled bodies were everywhere. A woman lay still, her arms still clutching a whimpering baby. People walked around, dazed. Some tried to help each other. The ground was turning red from blood. Another soldier came over to our group.

"If you can walk, try to get out of town now," he said.
"Go," the redheaded woman urged my friends, "I will take care of her."
"Yes, you must go," I agreed. We hugged each other.
"Goodbye," they whispered.
I watched them leave, stepping over bodies and scattered car parts. It was the last time I saw Elsa. Two days later her father, scared of the enemy that he was told would rape and torture women, shot Elsa, her mother, then himself. The young woman took my arm and led me down the street toward the first aid station.
"I heard your friends call you Elisabeth," she said. "My name is Anna."
There were others ahead of us at the first aid station. As we waited, I suddenly realized we were only a couple of streets from my father's home. So far, the house had escaped the bombs.
My head throbbed, but the pain in my heart was much worse. I missed my father terribly. If only he could be here and take me in his arms, if only I could be his little girl again. The last letter that I had received from him a few days earlier was weeks old. He was somewhere in Finland defending the fatherland, a fatherland that was all but destroyed. The letter was the last sign of life I would have from him for more than two years. His unit was captured by Russians just a few days later and taken to a Russian prison camp. He was held there for four and a half years.
A medic motioned me to a chair. He pulled the scarf off my throbbing head. Anna held my hand.
"You have a very deep cut," the medic said, "but there is not much we can do. We are running out of supplies." He cleaned the wound with disinfectant, put a strip of gauze over it, then covered my head with a bandage. He managed to grin and said, "You look like a mummy." Then he turned

to the young woman. "Take her south on this road until you come to a field. There is a foot path that will get you back to the highway, but you will be at least a mile out of town."

My new friend and I left. My head was still aching. The first aid station gave pain medicine only to the most seriously injured. They could do nothing else for me.

Soon we found the foot path across the field. Anna was from Berlin. Her husband was a military doctor. His last letter was sent from a military hospital in Backnang, a small town about twenty miles from us. He was afraid that he might never see her again, never hold her in his arms again. He, who had always been loyal to the Fuehrer, had lost hope for the future. Their chance for a happy life was destroyed and lay in rubble like their country. He was not sure if he would ever see Anna again.

That was when she decided to leave Berlin. Their home and all their worldly possessions were buried under tons of rubble. When she boarded the truck in Bad Cannstatt, she had been traveling nearly ten days by train, on foot, on trucks and refugee wagons. She was convinced the end of the world—she called it "Judgment Day"—would be here very shortly. She was going to find her husband and die with him.

The highway came in sight. Refugees sat at the side of the road, covered by dust from passing military vehicles. Others lumbered along, carrying their meager possessions. Anna and I kept heading northeast. I felt faint. The last food I ate was the watery breakfast soup at the school early that morning. My head was throbbing, and I felt hot.

A motorcycle roared past, a Red Cross flag flying from its handle bar. Right behind it came a truck clearly identified as a Red Cross vehicle by the Red Cross painted on its top and sides. Anna stepped out into the road and held up her hand. The truck stopped. Refugees stopped to watch, but none came near. The motorcycle turned around and came back. The door of the truck opened, an elderly sergeant stuck out his head.

"We need help," Anna said. "My friend was injured in a car wreck a few miles back."

"Get in," the sergeant yelled.

We climbed into the small back seat. The truck sped off, the motorcycle in front again. Two other soldiers shared the front seat with the sergeant, who was driving. The back of the truck was loaded with medical supplies for a field hospital in Loewenstein. They would take Anna to Backnang and then me within four miles of my grandparents' home, if they could get through.

"The stretch of highway we are on has been under air attack since early morning," the sergeant told us.

Even vehicles clearly identified as Red Cross had been shot at. Just at that moment, something roared overhead, immediately followed by the *ack-ack* of gunfire. The truck came to a screeching stop.

"Get into the ditch," the sergeant yelled and jumped out, followed by the other soldiers and Anna.

I could not move. The sergeant raced back, grabbed my arm, pulled me out and shoved me under some bushes in the ditch. Two planes dove low, shooting at us, then disappeared on the horizon. Thankfully, they missed us.

Everyone climbed back into the truck. The sergeant reached for a box in the back and dug out some pills.

"Here," he gruffly said to me, "this should help your pain."

Less than five minutes later a new wave of planes roared over us. We managed to jump out of the truck and hit the ditch before one of the planes dove down and shot at the vehicle. The windshield shattered, but no other damage was done. The planes disappeared again behind clouds.

Shaken, but unhurt, our group climbed out of the ditch. Then we saw them. Two soldiers, ropes around their necks, were hanging from a tree. Large cardboard signs around their necks read, "I am a coward and a deserter."

"Let's go," the sergeant said, "there is nothing we can do here."

We climbed back into the truck but again did not get very far before we were shot at again. I lay in the ditch, feeling numb from pain and shock. The pain pills helped a little, but I felt very hot.

The attacks lasted all afternoon. Again and again we hit the ditch. Other vehicles received direct hits and lay immobile in the highway. Our group was lucky. Even though the truck was riddled with bullet holes, the motor cranked every time we climbed back in. It took hours to cover the few miles to Backnang.

We arrived in Backnang in late afternoon, and the sergeant decided to look for shelter until dark. The streets were packed with refugees. Mud-caked soldiers pulled handcarts loaded with guns and backpacks through town. The truck stopped in front of a house.

The sergeant asked a man standing there where we might find a place to rest and wait until dark to continue our journey. The man offered us shelter in the cellar of his house. Anna was anxious to leave and got directions to the hospital. She hugged me tightly, then abruptly turned and left. I wanted to ask what her last name was, but Anna had already gone. Years later, I tried in vain to find this courageous woman. I never forgot her. I prayed that she found her husband and that together they found the peace and happiness they had dreamed of before their world fell apart.

The cellar was filled with refugees. I found a space on the floor and leaned my head against the stone wall. I dug into my bag and pulled out a small piece of my dried bread. A woman holding a child sat next to me on the floor. The little boy looked hungrily at the bread in my hand. No sound came from his lips. His eyes were not the eyes of a little child. They were eyes that had seen death, destruction and fire raining from the skies. Slowly, I reached for his hand and put the bread in it.

"God bless you," his mother whispered.

"Your God has run out of blessings," I whispered back. Tears trickled down the woman's face.

Air raid sirens screamed their warning outside. The sound of planes droned overhead. Footsteps cluttered down the cellar steps. Several SS soldiers barged into the already overflowing basement. One of their officers looked at the women and children huddled together in fear.

"Don't worry," he laughed confidently. "This war will be over very soon. Our Fuehrer has a new weapon. In just a few days, England will be destroyed. We will be victorious."

The owner of the house had also joined the group. "Yes," he agreed, "we already have new weapons. The soldiers outside are pulling them through town in little children's wagons. Just go up and see for yourself."

For a moment, there was dead silence. Then, in the blink of an eye, the SS officer pulled a revolver from his holster and pointed it at the man.

"Nobody will defame our Fuehrer, Adolf Hitler. Not while I and my comrades can still fight. You shall die for this, old man!"

Terror stricken, the man sunk to his knees. His skin was chalk white, his outstretched hands shaking uncontrollably.

"Please," he begged, "I was trying to make a joke. It did not mean a thing. I love the Fuehrer. Please let me live!"

"Come on, Hans," another officer stepped forward and put his hand on the SS officer's shoulder. "We have more important things to do. Let's go."

The officer put his pistol back into its holster. "Coward," he muttered. His spit, acid with contempt, hit the man's forehead. Seconds later, the soldiers ran up the cellar steps and disappeared.

Dusk slowly descended upon the town, finally turning to darkness, wrapping a temporary cloak of safety around a wretched people who had lost all hope. The sergeant was ready to leave. My head was throbbing again; the pain medicine was wearing off. Wearily, I climbed into the Red Cross truck.

I missed Anna sitting beside me. I wondered if she had found her husband in the chaos that prevailed around us.

"God, take care of her," I whispered.

God? Did I actually call on God, a God I was not sure existed? Early childhood memories crowded into my mind, Grandmother reading Bible stories to me, teaching me Scripture verses. I had not seen a Bible in years. None could be found in stores. One of our teachers said the only Bible we needed was Hitler's *Mein Kampf*, Hitler's autobiography, in which he stated his political ideas and plans for Germany.

I closed my eyes, shutting out shrouded images of refugees huddled together at the side of the road. The car groped its way through the darkness, guided only by two small shafts of light seeping through the covered headlights. It was nearly midnight when a light appeared on the road ahead, weaving back and forth, coming closer. The car stopped. A man, waving a flashlight walked up to the car. On the side of the road stood a pair of horses hitched to a wagon.

"You have to turn back," the man shouted. "All roads are closed."

"We have medical supplies for the field hospital in Loewenstein," the sergeant shouted back. "We have to get through."

"Loewenstein has been captured. The last we heard is that the field hospital has been moved to Wuestenrot, but nobody knows what is going on or if anyone is still alive there. We blocked the road halfway up the mountain with farm wagons, plows, trees and mines. That should stop whoever tries to come over the mountain road. You have to go back the way you came. It is the only road still open leading out from our village."

My mind churned. We were four kilometers from my grandparents' home. Grandpa had an eye operation recently and was still on sick leave from his railroad job. They needed me. Grandma could pray while I did more useful things like gather wood for cooking or hunt for food.

The sergeant, the soldiers and I climbed out of the truck.

"There must be a way to get these supplies to the hospital," the sergeant said.

"No," the farmer shook his head. "There is no other way over the mountain. Go back."

Since I was a little girl, I had spent part of every summer in Wuestenrot with my Aunt Karoline. I roamed the woods with the village children, picking blackberries, searching for mushrooms, chasing butterflies and watching the squirrels jump from tree to tree. We lay under trees on carpets of pine needles and watched the sun weave patterns of gold around us. We picked wild roses at the edge of the woods. In the meadows, we filled our arms with poppies, daisies and blue cornflowers.

Aunt Karoline put the roses in a crystal vase, the

wildflowers in an old milk jug. She said they were more beautiful than the expensive bouquets she received from admirers when she was a young girl. Then she invited us into the dining room and served us cookies and homemade raspberry juice, just as she did for her friends who visited on Sunday afternoons.

I knew every trail through the woods and meadows. I tugged at the sergeant's sleeve.

"There is an old wagon road going over the mountain, but you would never make it in a car."

The sergeant spun around. "Are you sure?"

"Yes, the road turns off into the woods just beyond the village."

"Could we get through with a wagon and horses?"

"I think so."

The sergeant reached back into the truck and pulled out a notepad. Hastily, he tore off a sheet of paper and scribbled something on it. He handed it to the farmer.

"This is a receipt for your horses and wagon," he said. "You will get them back or be reimbursed for them."

The farmer grabbed one of the horse's reins. "You can't take my horses and wagon," he shouted. "This is all I have left to work my fields. It is planting time. How will I plant my fields?"

"I am sorry," the sergeant answered. "Our Fuehrer would want you to help our fatherland, our soldiers. Lives depend on these medical supplies."

"The hell with our Fuehrer," the farmer shouted. "I already gave him one son. You can't take my horses."

"Unload the supplies and put them in the wagon," the sergeant commanded his men.

The farmer stepped back, tears trickled into his beard. Silently, he watched the men loading boxes into his wagon. The sergeant helped me onto the small seat.

"You have to show us the way," he said, taking the seat next to me.

The soldiers climbed into the back of the wagon. The farmer walked over and put his arms around the neck of one of the horses, burying his head deep into the soft mane. He reached down and removed the lantern hanging on the side of the wagon. Wordlessly, he handed it up to the sergeant.

"I need your flashlight too." The farmer handed up the flashlight.

"Don't worry about the horses," the sergeant said softly. "I was raised with horses, and I know how to drive a team. I will take good care of them."

With that, he took the reins and clicked his tongue. The horses pulled the wagon forward; the farmer disappeared behind us into the night.

Without my help, the soldiers would have missed the old wagon road leading off into the woods. Soon the trail became steeper and steeper. Dark woods surrounded us on both sides, pushing the trees closer and closer in the black night. A single star sent down a velvet thread of silver. Occasionally, a pale moon pushed the clouds aside, looked in astonishment upon the small group, then disappeared again. A cold wind blowing from the north made me pull my worn coat tighter around me. The horses strained in their harnesses, seeking sure footage on the rocky trail. The road disappeared into blackness.

"Stop," I finally said. "I think we can stay in the road if I walk ahead, but one of you will have to guide the horses."

The sergeant brought the horses to a halt, then handed me the flashlight. One of the soldiers jumped down and grabbed one of the horses by its halter. After a laborious climb, we reached the top of the mountain. I peered down into the darkness below us. The others joined me. No lights from the village below greeted us.

"Are you sure your grandparents' village is down there?" the sergeant asked.

"Yes," I answered. "Listen."

There were faint sounds, sounds of car engines and voices flung away by the wind. I shivered. How long had it been since English class this morning? Hours? Days? Months?

A familiar sound reached my ears. The clock in the church tower struck two. I smiled. Aunt Karoline had lived by the church bells and the church clock. They guided her life. She got up when the clock struck six in the morning, even if the snow was piled knee-deep around her house. By the strike of eight, the breakfast dishes were in the sink. Lunch was on the table before the clock had finished striking twelve noon.

Before the war, church bells were important for life in the village. They chimed on special holidays, for baptisms, weddings, funerals, and they called the congregation together every Sunday morning for worship service. The bells rang at sunrise and at sundown. The evening bell was the *Betglocke*, the prayer bell. Farmers stopped their work in the fields and gave thanks to the Lord who had protected them another day. Children everywhere would stop their games and go home for supper. To stay out after the *Betglocke* rang was a nearly unforgivable sin.

The ride downhill was much smoother. Before the church clock struck half past two, we were at the edge of the village. Sprinkles of lights appeared here and there. Feverish activity, noise and confusion were everywhere. Ambulances rumbled past; soldiers and civilians jammed the road. People stared at us.

"Where is the field hospital?" the sergeant shouted to a soldier.

"In the schoolhouse!" the soldier yelled back, then, looking at the back of the wagon, he crossed himself. "Praise the Lord! You got through with the medical supplies we need."

My grandparents' house was only yards from the schoolhouse. I climbed stiffly off the wagon. The sergeant handed my small bag to me.

"Thank you," he said, "the Fuehrer…"

"Please," I interrupted, "don't tell me the Fuehrer would be proud of me. Not today!"

"You are right. Have someone look at your head." He saluted, and the soldiers waved. Nobody said "Heil Hitler," the usual greeting for "hello" and "goodbye."

I stood in Grandma's yard. The front door opened, and two soldiers walked down the stone steps and passed me. Soldiers in Grandma's house? I slowly opened the front door. The kitchen door at the end of the hall stood ajar; so was the door to the living room. I could hear many voices. Was Grandma having a party?

As I passed the mirror in the hallway, I caught sight of a girl that I hardly recognized. An ashen face stared back at me. Bloody strands of my hair curled from beneath a blood-soaked bandage. The collar of my blouse was bloodstained, my skirt covered with mud.

I felt faint as I walked toward the kitchen door. Suddenly, there was my Oma hugging me, her tears mingling with the dried blood on my blouse. She pulled me into the kitchen. Grandpa stood at the old wood stove stirring something in a huge pot. Dark glasses covered his eyes.

I recognized two of the neighborhood women. Soldiers sat around the kitchen table, holding mugs of hot peppermint tea. Through the open living-room door, I saw a soldier sleeping on Grandma's couch, the couch that was reserved for Sunday afternoon guests only. Others slept in chairs or on the floor. A huge bowl of apples stood on the kitchen table, their sweet fragrance mingling with the mint. Grandpa dropped his spoon. He rushed over to me and pushed me into a chair.

"Dr. Lothar! Dr. Lothar," Grandma shouted up the stairs, "come quick! My granddaughter is here, and she needs help!" An officer, rubbing his eyes, rushed down the stairs. "I am sorry I had to wake you," Grandma apologized.

"That's all right," Dr. Lothar replied. "I have to get back to the hospital anyway. So, this is your granddaughter. Your grandparents have been worried sick about you, young lady. The roads to the west are closed. How did you get here?"

"We came over the mountain with a wagon load of medical supplies."

Dr. Lothar's eyes widened. "You came over the mountain with the Red Cross truck we thought was lost?"

"No, we came in a wagon with horses we stole from a farmer." It was hard to talk now. I wanted to lay down right in the middle of the hallway and sleep.

The doctor turned to Grandma. "I am taking her to the hospital, but I will bring her back soon. Please wake the boys and tell them we need everybody at the hospital immediately."

Gently, he took me by the arm and guided me out into the night. The street was still noisy, but now I heard a new sound. Gunfire!

The schoolyard was filled with vehicles, people and stretchers. Village women filled cups with coffee made from grain. I saw the horses and wagon at the front door, already emptied of their precious cargo. The sergeant and his soldiers were nowhere in sight.

Dr. Lothar guided me up the stairs and into the makeshift hospital. We walked through a hall filled with wounded soldiers and civilians sitting on the floor and lying on stretchers. He opened the door to one of the classrooms. I would have fainted had not the strong arm of the doctor held me up. Cots and stretchers were set up around the room. A young man sat on the first cot. Blood seeped through the bandage around his chest, his right arm hung uselessly down his side. He cried out in a language I could not understand.

"Ukrainian," Dr. Lothar said. "He calls for his mother."

Moans and cries came from other rooms where doctors, operating mostly without anesthesia, were frantically trying to save lives. Stretcher-bearers rushed in, carrying a barely-conscious elderly man. A militia armband on his sleeve showed that he, like many old men and young boys, had been pressed into service at the last minute to defend the Fatherland. I recognized the man, a farmer who lived in the next village. With glazed eyes, the man looked at his wife who ran alongside the stretcher, clutching his hand. Bloody intestines spilled from his body, staining his wife's dress crimson red and leaving a trail of death behind.

"I want to go home," I whispered. Gently, the doctor removed my blood-soaked bandage and snipped away at my hair. He poured a burning liquid on the wound, muttering to himself as he wrapped a clean bandage around my head.

"Someone will take you home," he assured me.

A little while later, I sat at my grandparents' kitchen table. Doctors and medics came and went all night. Grandma and Grandpa had opened their home to the exhausted soldiers. Grandpa cooked oatmeal on the old woodstove as long as his supply lasted, and Grandma made gallons of peppermint tea. Neighbor women brought apples and a few loaves of bread.

Grandpa made trip after trip down to the cellar to fill jugs with his famed apple cider from a large barrel. It bubbled like champagne. His secret ingredient was quince, grown on two trees in his orchard. The quince, he claimed, gave the cider a soft golden color and made it bubble like champagne.

Some of the soldiers were too tired to eat but snatched an hour or two of sleep in whatever space they could find in the house. Towards morning, the activity in the village increased. The gunfire was coming closer. At the break of dawn, an exhausted Dr. Lothar came back to the house.

"Everybody, wake up and go to the hospital immediately," he shouted. Soldiers staggered off the floors and rushed out. Dr. Lothar pressed a small vial of pills in Grandma's hand. "For Elisabeth," he said, "it might keep her from getting a fever." His eyes showed hopelessness and defeat. "We will leave in half an hour, please come with us. We are taking all women and children who want to go."

"No," Grandma responded, "we will stay."

Dr. Lothar did not pressure her. "Pray to your Lord to grant us safe passage, and pray that He will take care of you also."

Grandma's eyes grew sad. "I wish you knew my Lord," she said.

"A long, long time ago, in another lifetime, I thought I did. But he forgot about us, about the wounded, the suffering, the dying, or maybe he died also." He shook Grandpa's hand and hugged Grandma. "Thank you for opening your house and your heart to us."

We stood by the window as the convoy pulled out.

One by one, military vehicles and ambulances rolled by. A few women and children boarded a truck, each carrying a small bag. Soon the rumbling of motors stopped, the vehicles topped a hill and disappeared around a curve. The village street that was jammed with people just minutes before was nearly empty.

Grandma gathered pillows and blankets and carried them down to the cellar. Three old cots were set up in a corner. Grandpa put the last of the oatmeal in a bowl and wrapped some cheese from the last food ration in a cloth. I carried the can of tea and the leftover bread to our shelter. A corner shelf held several jars of canned, homegrown vegetables and fruits. We could survive for a few days. We made one last trip upstairs to fetch several suitcases and bags.

Suddenly there was shouting and yelling in the street. People, village people, neighbors, friends, had gone mad. They were looting a grocery store and a shoe shop nearby, grabbing what they could without looking at the merchandise. Since the shelves were already nearly empty, everything was gone in minutes. Stunned, my grandparents and I watched from a living room window. The gunfire intensified. People raced for their homes, their arms loaded with things, some items completely useless.

The three of us huddled around Grandpa's railroad lantern, which stood on an old rickety table emitting a small circle of light. Grandma's Bible lay on her knees, unopened. She did not need a light to read from it.

"*Der Herr ist mein Hirte; mir wird nichts mangeln.*" The Lord is my shepherd; I shall not want.

Outside, people shot at each other, killing and maiming. Were they all God's children? The German soldiers, the enemy soldiers, the thousands of women and children who had died during bombings, and the men who had dropped the bombs on them, were they all God's children? Was He the Shepherd of all of them?

My head started to hurt again. Dr. Lothar had said he once thought there was a God, a God who now had either abandoned us or had ceased to exist. I would stop thinking for now. Later I would ask Grandma or Grandpa about it.

Grandma gave me one of the pills Dr. Lothar had left. We ate cold oatmeal and drank cold peppermint tea. We were not sure how many hours had passed since the convoy had left that morning, since the people looted the stores, since the shooting had intensified.

I fell into a fitful sleep but awoke abruptly. Something was different. I listened and realized the shooting had stopped. There was an eerie silence. The world had come to a standstill. Then, we heard voices outside.

Grandma decided to go upstairs to see what was going on. Grandpa tried to talk her out of it, but she would not listen. I decided to go with her. Slowly we crept up the cellar stairs and inched our way into the living room. All curtains were closed tightly. We could still hear the voices outside. I recognized them as English.

"My English book may come in handy after all," I thought briefly.

Grandma went over to one of the windows and parted a curtain a little. She let it fall back into place and turned around. I will never forget this moment for the rest of my life. Grandma had the strangest expression on her face. It was absolute shock and disbelief. She tried to say something but could not.

I leaned against the wall. I was so scared that I could not move. I knew Grandma must have seen something even more horrible than what we were told to expect. For weeks, we were told that enemy soldiers would rape the women, kill the children and old men and burn what little the people had left.

Grandma turned back to the curtain, parted it again and looked out once more. Then she turned back, still looking as if she could not believe what she had just seen.

"Elisabeth," she whispered, "they are just people like we are."

The front door was kicked open. Soldiers pointed rifles at us through the living room door. For a moment, there was stark fear.

"Are you hiding soldiers or guns in the house?" a man in a strange-looking uniform barked.

"No," I replied, "we have no guns and the only man in the house is my grandfather who just had eye surgery. He is down in the cellar."

"You speak English?"

"Yes."

One of the soldiers came into the living room. He walked over to the piano, opened the lid and ran his fingers over the keys. He grinned and sat down, propping his gun against the side of the piano. His hands flew over the keyboard.

"I am working on the railroad," he sang. The others joined in. Then they left as fast as they had come.

Slowly, people emerged from their hiding places. My grandparents and I joined some of our neighbors outside. My head was wrapped in a scarf, hiding the bandage. I felt better. Dr. Lothar's pills had helped.

Three of my girlfriends joined me. We watched soldiers in tanks and jeeps roll by, soldiers who waved and yelled "Hello, *Fraeulein!*" Other soldiers walked next to the vehicles. Some stopped and gave candy and chewing gum to the children. They looked at it wide-eyed, not sure what to do. One soldier kneeled down in front of a little boy. He blew a big bubble from his mouth and made it pop.

The child looked at him with big, solemn eyes.

"Bubble gum," the soldier said and handed him a piece. "You try it."

The child put the gum in his mouth. He started to chew it, then promptly swallowed it.

"*Nein, nein,*" the soldier exclaimed. "Blow it, don't swallow it. Here are two more. Try it again." He stood up, waved to the boy and moved on down the street.

Suddenly, a jeep drove up the short drive to my grandparent's house. Three soldiers and an officer jumped out, cradling guns in their arms.

"Is this your house?" the officer asked in perfect German.

"Yes, it is," Grandpa answered.

"You have ten minutes to vacate the premises. You may take what you can carry," he barked.

Grandma, who until that minute had been a pillar of strength, started to cry. "Where shall we go?"

"Ask your *Ortsgruppenleiter* (the town's Nazi leader)," came the short reply.

I was the first to recover from this unexpected turn of events. I raced down to the cellar and groped around in the dark until I found the two water buckets full of sugar Grandma had been hiding. We knew that Grandma had bought it on the black market, but she would never tell what she paid or traded for it. Sugar was nearly worth its weight in gold.

When I reached the yard, Grandma was crying in Grandpa's arm. The officer leaned against a wall of the house. He looked at his wristwatch.

"Five minutes," he said.

Neighbors struggled up the street, carrying suitcases and bags. A few carried bedding. One woman carried her cat. They all had been ordered out of their houses. Those who had looted the stores had to leave their stolen treasures behind.

"Where are you going?" I asked nobody in particular.

"To the cave in the woods," the woman with the cat answered.

I raced back down to the cellar and grabbed two small suitcases. When I came back up the officer shouted, "Your time is up!"

Grandma stood in the middle of the yard, alone.

"Where is Grandpa?" I asked in panic.

"He went back into the house to get something. He said for us to go on. He will be right behind us."

I grabbed the sugar buckets, and Grandma took the two small suitcases. As we walked down the driveway, flanked by thick hedges, soldiers rushed past us, going to the house. We had nearly reached the road when gunfire erupted again.

"Luise, Elisabeth," Grandpa shouted from the doorway. "Come back, come to the cellar!"

Windows crashed. Shells hit the side of the house, the roof, and nearby trees. Several of the soldiers rushed to the house and followed Grandpa inside. They had understood the German word *Keller*, which sounded nearly like cellar. They knew it would offer safety. Others ducked behind hedges and behind the small wall next to the front steps.

Grandma and I hit the ground next to the lilac bush. Aunt Karoline had planted it many years ago. The bush was already in full bloom. I looked up into its branches. Had there ever been such beautiful purple blossoms and emerald leaves before? No, these flowers were the most beautiful I had ever seen the bush bloom. Inhaling deeply the delicate fragrance, I hoped that none of the shells would hit the bush and shred its flowers and leaves.

The shooting seemed to come from nearby. Soldiers

shouted orders in the street. Nobody seemed to know what was going on. Just as suddenly as it had started, the shelling stopped. As we stood up, we heard the front door open. Three German soldiers, their hands held high over their heads, emerged. They were prodded by four American soldiers who pushed their guns into the Germans' backs. Behind them was Grandpa, his face chalk white. His shaking hands held the lit railroad lantern. Nobody paid him any attention, neither the German prisoners nor the American soldiers.

Later, when we reached the safety of the cave in the woods, Grandpa told us what happened. He could hear people following him down the cellar steps. He thought Grandma and I were following him. He struck a match and lit the lantern. To his horror, he saw three German soldiers in front of him and four American soldiers behind him. The Germans must have been hiding at the far end of the orchard and apparently entered the cellar while the house was being evacuated.

Whatever their intentions were could not be determined any more. Maybe they wanted to find shelter when the shelling started, or maybe they wanted to make a last stand against the enemy. Everyone was stunned. The Americans recovered first. They pointed their guns at the German soldiers and took them prisoners. The Germans seemed relieved that the war was nearly over for them.

The cave was crowded. I slept on my stomach with my arms around the sugar buckets, one on each side of me. I was too tired to feel the damp, hard cave floor.

A glorious sun arose the next morning. People sat outside the cave. Small children played with sticks and pebbles, inventing their own games. Around noon, three German soldiers in tattered uniforms emerged from the steep ravine beside the cave. When they reached the top, they collapsed from exhaustion and hunger. Their weapons lay at the bottom of the ravine, lost during their arduous climb.

A woman fetched water from a nearby creek; another brought a few slices of bread. Someone produced a bottle of wine and salami to share with the men. They had been separated from their unit and were hiding at the bottom of the ravine all night. Now they were unsure what to do.

"Take off your uniforms and throw them back into the ravine," an old man said.

Somehow, the villagers came up with enough old clothes for the three men. The war was over for them. All they wanted now was to go home.

Sounds drifted up from the village. Vehicles drove back and forth. The guns were silent now. The shooting had stopped. After three days, everything turned quiet. No voices, no cars, no sounds at all could be heard from the village.

The farmers wanted to go back home to take care of their cows and horses. Three villagers set out as scouts. They soon returned. The village was vacated; the American soldiers were gone. Nobody knew if the war was over, if there was still a German army, if Hitler was still alive. Most of the people were farmers. Their animals had to be taken care of, their fields had to be planted. Life had to go on.

Cautiously, people walked back to the village, families staying close together. I carried my sugar buckets. The front door of our house stood wide open. Cautiously, we stepped into the hallway. As we entered the living room, we stopped. We could not believe what we saw. The dining table was loaded with food. There were cans of food, bread so white that it looked like cake and even several packs of cigarettes. Much later, I found out that the food was C-rations the soldiers carried with them in combat. Most of it was unfamiliar to us. There were baked beans, deviled hams, spam and other unfamiliar delicacies we had never seen before or had forgotten about. There was candy, chocolate bars and chewing gum. It was a miracle.

Grandpa ran across the yard to the neighbors, who also were transplanted city people and without the food that was still available to the farmers. "Come to our house," he yelled. "We have food!"

A woman, her eyes shining, emerged from the house. She clutched a loaf of bread to her breast. "We too have food," she yelled back.

One by one, people came from the house carrying small cans of food, loaves of bread and chocolate bars. The children clutched candy in their small hands. They followed Grandpa back to our house and put their food on the table, adding it to the bounty already there. They opened the cans and passed them around. We ate in silence.

Minutes passed, fifteen minutes or more. Then everyone started to talk and laugh at once. Grandpa went down to the cellar and fetched a pitcher of his famous apple cider. He poured the golden liquid into glasses and passed them around. Everyone raised their glasses high and made a toast to the unknown men who made this feast possible. A young woman went to the piano and started to play. Tables and chairs were pushed against the wall.

"May I have this dance?" Grandpa bowed gracefully to Grandma, put his arm around her waist and whirled her around.

We laughed, sang, danced and ate way into the night. Whatever was going on in other parts of the world at that moment, we did not care about it. For us, the war was over. For the first time in many, many months our stomachs were full. We had no running water, no electricity. It did not matter.

Grandma put candles around the room and drew water from the well in the yard to brew pot after pot of peppermint tea while Grandpa kept the cider glasses filled. It was to be many months, for some of us years, until our stomachs were full again.

We heard little news from the outside world. Newspapers had stopped printing. Electricity was shut off and if available, turned on for only two or three hours during the day. Most radios were destroyed, and there was no mail service. Rumors abounded, rumors that the German Army had won new victories with secret weapons, or that the Allied troops were crushing the country and that Hitler was dead. Fear crept back into people's hearts.

The main source of news, local or national, came from the *Buettel*, the town crier. He carried a large hand bell and sheets of papers with mostly handwritten notes. He stopped at certain places around the village. One of his stopping places was by the well in Grandpa's front yard. There, he rang his bell and shouted the news. But even he was silent now.

Then, in the middle of May, his bell rang again. People rushed from their houses to hear the news. On April 30th, ten days after his fifty-sixth birthday, Adolf Hitler had committed suicide in his bunker in Berlin. The day before, he had appointed Grand Admiral Karl Doenitz as his successor. Early on May 7th, 1945, General Alfred Jodl, as the representative of Doenitz, signed the unconditional surrender of Germany at Eisenhower's headquarters in Reims, France. The war was over.

Elfriede E. Wilde

VOLKSSTURM MILITIA

In spring of 1945, shortly before the end of the war, males between the ages of thirteen and sixty who were not already serving in the military or some other organization for Germany's defense, were drafted into the *Volkssturm*. This organization was a militia, and even twelve-year-olds volunteered. It was a last effort to hold back enemy soldiers who had already entered German territory in the East and West. No uniforms were issued, only black armbands identifying members of the *Volkssturm*.

My friend Erwin, fifteen years old, lived close to my grandparents. He and several other boys were ordered to report to city hall, wearing their Hitler Youth uniforms. They were assigned to a nearby military unit and received minimal instructions in using a bazooka. Less than a week later, most of the soldiers, including Erwin and four other teens, were captured by American soldiers and marched back to the village. The five boys were separated from the German soldiers and by some coincidence brought to my grandparents' house, a house Erwin knew very well. The boys, in mud-caked and tattered Hitler Youth uniforms, squeezed together on my grandma's couch.

A guard stood at the open door of the living room. After a while, a tall black soldier walked in, carrying several small, opened cans. He handed a can to each of the boys. Looking at the unknown contents, they did not know what to do.

Finally, the soldier said in a loud commanding voice, "Eat!"

The boys, scared and unable to understand the foreign word, sat there unmoving. After repeating the command several times, the soldier reached into his shirt pocket and pulled out a small book which must have been a tiny dictionary. He leafed through it, finally finding the German word for eat.

"*Essen*," he commanded two or three times.

The boy sitting next to Erwin nudged him and whispered, "Don't eat it; it could be poison."

The boys had not eaten in nearly two days, and even before that their rations were restricted. They were very hungry. Carefully, Erwin stuck a finger into the can, then licked it. Whatever it was, it tasted wonderful. He decided that to die of poison would be more pleasant than to die of starvation. Using his fingers, he scooped out the food and devoured it in seconds. The smiling soldier handed him another can, then watched as the others followed suit. The soldier gathered up the empty cans and handed each of the boys a small chocolate bar.

Later in the afternoon they loaded into a truck and rode to a large building in Weinsberg. Erwin thought it was a former schoolhouse. They ate supper from cans, but again Erwin did not know what kind of food it was. They bedded down on the floor in one of the rooms. The same black soldier from earlier came back and brought them two rough military blankets.

The next day, they were roused very early and marched down the hall to another room. The soldier, who apparently had made it his mission to take care of the boys, again brought several cans of food and sliced bread. The bread looked like cake to them. They ate every morsel of the canned food, then stuffed as much bread as they could in their pants pockets.

After a while, one of the boys noticed that the door to the room was ajar. They looked at each other, went to the door, opened it slowly and looked out into the hall. The main entrance was only steps away. They reached it in seconds—it also was unlocked. On purpose?

They quietly slipped out and raced toward the nearby woods. They shed their jackets with the Hitler Youth insignias and threw them under some bushes. Their ragged and dirty pants were not recognizable as part of uniforms. They started on the twenty-kilometer trek home. The bread that they had stuffed into their pants that morning kept them from getting hungry. Everyone arrived safely at their parents' homes. They had survived.

THE CROSS

Years ago, the cross hung on the wall of the kindergarten room. Then, one day it was replaced with a large photo of Adolf Hitler, the Fuehrer of Germany. It was carelessly laid aside and could have ended up in the trash had not Lydia, the kindergarten teacher, picked it up. Nobody cared what happened to it.

About four days after I arrived at my grandparents' home, Stuttgart was captured and occupied by invading enemy soldiers. During the next ten days, nearly fourteen hundred women were raped by invading enemy soldiers (Hosseinzadeh, 32-33). Chaos prevailed.

Lydia remembered the cross she had saved so long ago. She lived in the same house where my girlfriend lived with her parents and several other families. Hastily, she attached the cross to the front door, a door that could have easily been broken down.

Women in the houses on either side were raped, but no enemy soldier entered the house with the cross on the door.

Elfriede E. Wilde

A HERO

MAJOR WILLIAM PRESTON
2nd Commander of the 3rd Battalion
397th Infantry Regiment, 100th Division
1945

He had several names, the Savior of Weissach, the "gentle" Conqueror (Stuttgart Newspaper 31 December 1997, Das Portraet), and the builder of the chapel in the horse stables in the *Reiterkaserne*. But he did not want to be called a hero.

I visited my hometown Stuttgart, Germany, in summer 1992. Like always during my visits, I spent several days in the state library doing genealogical research. While searching for ancestors in the small town of Unterweissach, today Weissach im Tal, I came across a town history by Max Zuern. He vividly described the occupation by American forces on April 20, 1945:

It was a radiant morning. The trees were blooming, and the meadows emitted spring fragrances. As the valley opened up before the commander of the advance guard, he seemed to have been so surprised by the beauty of the country side that he gave the order 'Hold your fire! We will not shoot here!' He would keep his word. It was the 3rd Battalion of the 397th Regiment. Until today, this officer is unknown. He would still deserve our heartfelt thanks. (Zuern, 320)

When I returned to America, I could not get the story about the man who saved the village of my ancestors from certain destruction out of my mind. I searched in libraries and archives and talked by telephone with several offices in Washington, D.C. At that time, the Internet was still in its infancy. Research had to be done in person, by mail or by telephone. Very few people were knowledgeable in computer technology, and not even many businesses had computers. I found that the 3rd Battalion of the 397th Infantry Regiment, which belonged to the 100th Infantry Division, indeed came through Unterweissach.

Finally, on May 29th, 1993, I had a name. A telephone information operator gave me an address and a phone number in Burlington, Vermont. Again, at this time, I would not have been able to find this information on the Internet. I needed the assistance of a telephone information operator. For a moment, the man on the other end of the line was speechless when I told him why I called. Yes, he was the former Major William Preston, second in command of the battalion. He remembered the valley and the beautiful bridge in the middle of the village, and that they were able to take it without a fight. Many phone calls followed this first one, and soon we exchanged letters.

Major Preston told me that his unit arrived in Stuttgart by the end of April but could not stay there very long because the French took over the city. However, in July, the French gave back the city to the Americans, and Major Preston arrived again with his soldiers in Stuttgart. They were quartered in the *Reiterkaserne* (cavalry barracks), which was established for German cavalry long before World War I. Major Preston began to remodel a horse stable into a chapel where they held regular services.

The winter of 1945-46 was a very harsh and snowy winter in Stuttgart. The young soldiers who were allocated to drive Major Preston's jeep were all from the southern United States. Most saw snow for the first time in their lives. The art of driving under such conditions eluded them. Much to their embarrassment, Major Preston, who was used to driving in snow in his native Vermont, took over the wheel and relegated them to the passenger seat. Thus, the drives down the hill to Cannstatt were completed without serious incidents.

The soldiers named the *Reiterkaserne* Fort Henderson, or just "The Fort." A service club was established, also a movie theater called the Blue Theater; and on weekends, sports were played in the Century Stadium.

Immediately after my first telephone conversation with William Preston, I wrote a letter to Rainer Deuschle, mayor of Weissach im Tal, to inform him that I had found the officer involved in saving the valley and village from certain destruction. He and Joerg Zuern, son of Max Zuern who had authored the first town history, immediately contacted Major Preston. Mayor Deuschle wrote that because of the humane decision back then, his town had a positive development and was in a much better economic situation than some neighboring towns that were badly damaged or destroyed and had to rebuild. Weissach was spared this.

In 1995, Weissach im Tal celebrated its 750th anniversary. Mr. Preston, his wife Janet and I, were invited to a celebration in the *Seeguthalle*, a large town hall, on May 24, 1995. On May 21, my girlfriend Margit and I met the couple at the Stuttgart-Echterdingen airport and took them to the Hotel Rieker. The next day was spent sightseeing under the guidance of Margit.

The very first place we went to was the *Reiterkaserne*. Major Preston related the story of the remodeling of the horse stable to a chapel. He said that he wanted to create a place of peace where his soldiers could feel that God was still close, even if it was in a horse stable. He was much surprised by the beauty of the *Schlossplatz*, the castle square in the middle of the town. Back then, he told his wife that it was "*all kaput.*" He could not remember any flowers in the gardens, only the ruins of the destroyed New Castle, the *Koenigsbau* and the damaged Old Castle. That evening, we went to the Blockhaus for supper, a restaurant across the street from the train station. Unfortunately, they did not serve *knackwurst* and *sauerkraut*, Mr. Preston's favorite German dish that he remembered from 1945. Margit's husband, Juergen, ensured that it was served at his house the very next evening.

On May 24, Margit drove Major Preston, Janet and me to Weissach im Tal. There, we were invited for the customary afternoon coffee with the mayor, Juerg Zuern, their wives and a few city councilmen. Nobody else knew of our presence in town, nor that the officer who saved the town fifty years ago had been found. It was to be the big surprise for the evening festivities in the *Seeguthalle*.

The hall was filled to the last seat; many people from Stuttgart were also there. The mayor recalled the early beginnings of the town and continued through its history until he came to the happenings of April 1945. He read the article from the town history and then came the words, "The officer has been found, and he is here with us today." These words were our cue to go to the stage.

It felt like electricity had hit the hall. The standing ovation seemed never-ending. People cried. Even today, I cannot fully describe the emotions of that moment.

Mayor Deuschle said later, "We had chills run up and down our spines."

Major Preston gave a short speech which I translated. He said that he was fully convinced that God's spirit was at work on that fateful day in April 1945. He refused to be called a hero. Then, Mayor Deuschle presented him with the town's Medal of Honor and a certificate stating the reason for the presentation.

The evening ended with a big reception and huge fireworks. Among the countless people who came to shake William Preston's hand were many young Weissach residents who thanked him. They pointed out that their grandparents or parents might have been killed that day had it not been for Mr. Preston's decision.

The rest of the Prestons' stay in Stuttgart was mostly dedicated to sightseeing and re-discovering places that

Major Preston remembered. Margit was the tour guide. Major Preston was overwhelmed by the culture and the rebuilt city that lay in ruins the last time he was there. A few days later, Margit and I took the couple to the airport for their return trip to the United States. Another surprise waited. A Weissach delegation came to the airport to see them off.

In the fall of 1945, the book *Regiment of the Century: The Story of the 397th Infantry Regiment* was published in Stuttgart. It was written and illustrated by soldiers of the unit. In the foreword, they wrote that a bombed and nearly completely destroyed printing shop put up their presses and printed the book. The shop was the Union Druckerei (Union Printers) in Stuttgart.

I saw Major Preston and his wife, Janet, for the last time in September 1997 in Charlotte, NC, at the 100th Infantry Division's reunion. Preston's daughter, Betsy, brought her parents from Vermont to Charlotte, North Carolina. Due to a stroke, Major Preston was confined to a wheelchair.

My husband and I also were invited to attend. During the reunion festivities, Major Preston donated the Weissach Medal of Honor, in remembrance and in honor of all his comrades, to the Fort Jackson Museum in Fort Jackson, S.C. Fort Jackson was the "birthplace" of the 100th Infantry Division. The museum is an additional training center for new recruits, and the material will be used by researchers, scholars and historians. The medal represents appreciation for a humane act of compassion and shows how a difficult situation can be mastered. The medal will always be in the Ft. Jackson Museum, but actually is the property of the U.S. History Center of Military History in Washington, D.C.

I also received a surprise at the Charlotte reunion.

Major Preston received a special honor there, and I received one because I searched for him. After the banquet, many of the former soldiers came to shake my hand and thanked me for searching for Major Preston. They said it was a final healing between two countries that once fought each other. For me, it was the final end of the chaos of the war.

The town of Weissach im Tal later published a new town history. One chapter is dedicated to Major Preston with an account of his visit to the town fifty years after he and his troops saved Unterweissach from destruction.

CHAPTER THREE

NEW BEGINNINGS

Those who lived under Hitler's regime, who lived through the war and survived, will never forget it. They will never forget the death and destruction, the horrors, the starvation, the burial of their souls. Many suppressed the memory for a while, sometimes for years, but none could forget. For many, the end of the war was the end of their world. They had followed a leader who promised them the world, and they lost everything.

Others were just relieved that the bombings had stopped. There were streetlights now, no more blackouts. They did not have to sleep in their clothes in case of an air raid anymore. Starving and clad in rags, they stood before the ruins and next to hastily dug graves and doubted that new life could rise again from the ashes. Then slowly, they began sifting through the debris and salvaged what they could.

They lived in the rubble of their destroyed houses, in wet basements, in rooms with no windows, water seeping through broken walls and ceilings. They guarded their broken doors against intruders who wanted to steal their last slice of bread or the last potato they had left. They struggled fiercely for life's barest necessities. But there was a flicker of hope for a new beginning and a new life.

Shortly after the war ended, my mother also moved back to my grandparents' house for a while. Things did not get better for years. In fact, food became even more scarce after Germany was occupied by the Allied forces. The winters of 1946 and 1947 were the coldest in decades. Ice formed even on the inside of walls in houses. Many people, especially the old and the very young, died from the cold and malnutrition.

The most important things were food, shelter and clothing. Like many others, my mother and I applied for permits to gather brushwood, twigs and small limbs that had fallen from trees in the forest. This material was all we had for cooking and heating. Sometimes we could buy wood from farmers. We had to saw it into smaller pieces, then split it with an ax. A few times, we even stole a few pieces of cord wood that farmers stacked in the forest. We hated to do it, but the warm kitchen on a freezing winter evening felt great.

At harvest time, we asked for permits to glean the fields for fallen grain after the farmers had harvested. There were other families gleaning, and at the end of the day, I doubt that there was even one grain left on the ground for the birds. The grain was taken to a collecting station where it was weighed. We then received a few handfuls of flour. We spent days collecting beechnuts. Tired, dirty and hungry, we turned those in at the end of each day at another collecting station for a few tablespoons of oil.

Dandelions made a wonderful salad, nettles, picked young, were cooked like spinach, and sorrel added flavor to watery potato soups. My mother, who knew every edible mushroom and every edible weed and berry, taught me how to recognize them too. There was mint and yarrow for tea. Apple peelings added to rose hip also made a good tea. We picked wild blackberries, strawberries and blueberries. Plum seeds could be cracked so that we could eat the little stone inside the seed. I am convinced that some of these foods not only kept us from starving but actually kept us healthy.

Gas and electricity were still in short supply. People

remembered their grandma's *Kochkiste*, a cooking box dating back to the late nineteenth century. We found one in Aunt Karoline's attic. My grandfather remembered that she used it often when he was a little boy. It saved electricity. The *Kochkiste* became popular during WWI, then people rediscovered it again during WWII.

The box consisted of sturdy wood with a tight lid. It was lined and partially filled with straw or newspapers. Two holes were cut in the middle, large enough to put two pots into it. Grandpa painted Aunt Karoline's old box bright yellow and put it in their kitchen. A cooking pot with a tightly fitting lid was filled with rice, potatoes or other vegetables, and sometimes even meat if it was available. The food was cooked for about one-sixth of its regular cooking time, then put into the box with the wooden lid tightly closed. My mother explained that the pot should only be filled to two-thirds of its capacity to keep in the heat. It worked, and after several hours the food was cooked and ready to serve.

We took down the window curtains in my grandparents' little country home. One of my mother's friends was a seamstress who made skirts from the curtains. She also sewed a sheet into "blouse jackets" for us. My mother found a few scraps of embroidery thread and embroidered the pockets on the jackets, and we were very fashionable.

We converted a tablecloth into a skirt. Old sweaters that could not be mended anymore were unraveled. The yarn was wound around beer bottles and put over a pot of boiling water or food cooking on an old wood stove. The steam smoothed out the wool and made it possible to be re-knitted into sweaters, socks or caps. Worn or torn collars and cuffs on shirts and blouses were removed, turned over and re-attached. Threadbare sheets were cut apart in the middle and sewn back by putting the edges together.

Soap powder had long disappeared. All we had was a brown soap of very poor quality. It was used for washing clothes and for personal hygiene. Most of the washing was done with cold water. Clothes and linens had to be scrubbed with harsh brushes to remove dirt and spots. This scrubbing resulted in more and more threadbare clothing that could not be replaced.

Food was always scarce. We still had ration cards for several years after the war ended. Having a ration card did not guarantee that the food allocated was available in stores. Sometimes the store owner did not receive the food; sometimes it was sold out in minutes after the store opened. The last item on ration cards was sugar, which was rationed until 1950.

One way to obtain food, clothing, shoes and other necessary items was through the flourishing black market, or trade with other people. The black-market currency was called "cigarette currency" because nearly everything could be bought with cigarettes, especially American cigarettes. My mother was afraid to deal with people at the black market. She went a few times, but she would rather bargain and trade with farmers. She managed to save most of her jewelry during the war by wearing it, carrying it in a purse slung over her shoulders or hiding it inside her bra. Farmers were happy to trade for it.

Towns offered classes on how to recognize edible plants and how to cook them. My mother attended many of these classes, but many of her recipes were her own inventions. Here are some of her handwritten notes I found in one of her cook books after her death:

1945 - doctor had no medicine besides aspirin. I traded

bookmarks I painted for two oranges and two chocolate bars with an American soldier. I had forgotten what oranges are.

1945 - spring rations for one week - 1700 grams of bread, 250 grams of meat, 125 grams of fat.

1945 - rations for three weeks - 375 grams of sugar, 125 grams of cottage cheese, 62.5 grams of cheese, 225 grams of noodles or rice, 100 grams of substitute coffee (made from grain).

1946 - ration for one month - 250 grams of sugar, 700 grams of meat, 350 grams of fat. Horsemeat is sold for half ration, but one must stand in line for hours.

1947 - 50 grams of fat for one month
(1 ounce - 28.35 grams)

We supplement ration card food allowances with dandelions, nettles, sorrels, wild berries, mushrooms, and gather beechnuts. I applied for permit to glean in fields and to gather brush wood.

A few of my mother's handwritten recipes:

Spread for bread
1 tablespoon grease, any kind
2 tablespoons of flour
1 cup water (or part milk if available)
Pinch of salt
In small pan, brown flour in grease, add water and salt and beat with whisk
Add tomatoes or chives if available and spread on bread.

Sweet spread
Gather spoiled apples and pears in the field. They can have spots, mold, be brown or black. Squeeze through cheesecloth with a little water. Cook, bring to a boil and

cook until it has spreading consistency. Put in jars or crock and keep in cool cellar. Will keep about two weeks.

To stretch butter
Take about 30 grams of butter, add ½ liter skim milk (or half water) and 50 grams of flour and mix well. Bring to a boil until it gets thick. Chives can be added if desired. Let cool.

Another spread
Roast oats in a dry skillet (no fat needed), dissolve one Maggi (Bouillon) cube in a little water, add to the oats and stir until thick. Add caraway spice or a spoon of mustard.

How to preserve blueberries
Pick wild blueberries, wash well, put in empty beer bottles, close tops, put in kettle and process for 20 to 30 minutes at 80 degrees Celsius.
(Note added in 1947 - does not work, bottle exploded when opened).

Mushrooms
Bring to boil half vinegar and half water, salt, pepper and a bay leaf. Add sliced mushrooms and a few thinly sliced onion pieces. Boil for a few minutes. This can be put in glass jars and covered with paper and put in cool cellar. Will keep several days
(mushrooms dried in the sun will keep longer).

Cow beet syrup
Buy or trade with a farmer for cow beets. Wash, cut into small pieces, put in a pot and barely cover with water. It is best to do this in winter on a stove when there already is a fire to warm the room. The smallest amount used should be

as much as would fit into two large soup pots. Cook until you can squeeze the pieces with your fingers and they fall apart. Then squeeze through a cloth and cook the mass until it has the consistency of honey. One can tell this when the syrup turns brown and foams. As soon as foam builds, be very careful, because it could stick to the bottom of the pot and scorch. Too much stirring is not desirable, not until the end when the foam really foams. Put in jars and cover.

The blueberry explosion was a disaster. It happened in Grandma's kitchen. After the bottle exploded, juice and berries covered the ceiling, creating intricate blue designs.

My mother calmly looked at the ceiling and said, "Well, I believe we now have to live with a Picasso for a while."

Paint was not easily available during this time. It took nearly two years until Grandma found someone to paint her kitchen. I actually was a little sorry to see Picasso disappear.

Another disaster in Grandma's kitchen was the frog disaster. Green frogs, as well as vineyard snails, also helped us survive these years of starvation. Due to my parents' part-time residence in France before the war, they both had been familiar with these delicacies. Of course, in France they went to restaurants and ordered the ready-cooked meal. Such a luxury was not possible now, and other means to obtain frogs or snails had to be used. It was not unusual to get a group of friends together late at night to go frog-hunting in a nearby lake.

The frogs were easily caught at night. They were transported home in small milk cans with lids. Each cans held about two liters of liquid, enough space for about two dozen frogs. One night we brought home two cans of frogs. My mother always took care of the preparation, but she was too tired that evening to do anything. She left the live frogs in the cans with the lids slightly ajar for air. When we came downstairs next morning, unusual sounds greeted us. Grandma had gotten up earlier, felt sorry for the frogs and removed the lids. About four dozen frogs scampered around the kitchen. They were perched on tables and chairs, jumped from the top of the kitchen cabinet onto the sink, hid under the stove and got under our feet, putting on a frog concert. It took days to clear Grandma's kitchen of frogs.

One of Grandma's farm friends had a French worker helping with the farm work. Since my mother spoke perfect French, he was able to instruct her how to prepare both snails and frogs for human consumption. Thankfully, I never had to watch this, but we all enjoyed these occasional special treats.

My mother struggled to keep up the appearance of normal living. Every day, the table was set carefully for every meal, regardless how little there was to eat. Even though most of the dishes were mismatched and chipped, there were always fresh flowers or some green boughs in a vase on the table—usually wildflowers like daisies, cornflowers and poppies, or even blooming weeds picked in a field. Manners were also very important. My mother did not easily forgive someone's rudeness.

But there also were other times. We had lost nearly everything and had survived total destruction. Even though food was scarce, alcohol was usually available from farmers. People, mostly young people, started to celebrate. There were parties, dances and celebrations. We had hope again for a better tomorrow. Why not enjoy life? We were survivors.

Refugee families and German soldiers clad in rags, some of them near starvation, came walking through the village. Sometimes, a farmer would take in a family or give them some food, but most of them struggled on, hoping to start a new life.

A man in a tattered army uniform was given a tiny, unheated and sparsely-furnished attic room in the house next to us. He was an educated man, a university professor in civilian life, with impeccable manners. He was also destitute and separated from his family. He did not know what had become of them or if they were still alive. One day, he knocked at our door. My mother was an accomplished piano player, and he had listened to her music through our open window. He introduced himself, complimented her on her talents, kissed her hand, enchanted her and was invited into the house.

One day, we stumbled onto a large grove of beautiful mushrooms in the forest. We gathered as many as we could. We planned to dry some for winter, but some we cooked as soon as we arrived at home. My mother was an ingenious cook; somehow, she always managed to make things taste good. Besides picking wild herbs in forests and meadows, she also planted parsley, chives, rosemary and other herbs in Grandma's garden; and she could do wonderful things with them.

I remember the mushroom dinner we had that day. Somehow, my mother created a delicious sauce to go with the mushrooms and the few potatoes we had left. Red wine sparkled in mismatched glasses. Then she sent me to our neighbor, the professor, to invite him to share our meager meal. It was a wonderful, lighthearted meal with good conversation and laughter. I noticed that at the end of the meal the professor stared at his plate. We had finished all the mushrooms and all the potatoes. There was only a little sauce left in his plate. I had the feeling if we would have had bread, he would have dipped up the rest of the sauce with it, but we had no bread.

Suddenly, with a twinkle in his eyes, he picked up the plate with both hands and said, "We once had a maid and this is how she always finished her meals." Then he raised the plate to his mouth and licked the plate clean. Not even a drop was wasted.

And then there were the "Ami Boys," the American soldiers, who wore clean uniforms and were well-nourished. One day, one of my friends, a scrawny, malnourished young girl clad in rags, declared she had enough—enough of starvation, enough of tattered clothing and shoes with holes in the soles. She wanted to go dancing in a party dress and eat until her stomach was full. So, she took things into her own hands. She found an "Ami" boyfriend. Soon, she could trade American cigarettes on the black market for food for her entire family, and she wore nylon stockings and went to dances in a party dress.

HOBO   JESTER

PUPPETS AND FLOWERS WITH ROOTS

The first newspapers in our area were printed again in early fall of 1945, usually only twice a week. My mother sent me to everyone she knew who was able to buy a newspaper to ask them if she could have the used papers. I had to shred them into small pieces. Grandfather still had some glue from his furniture projects. My mother made a paste from glue and water and added the shredded newspapers. A friend made small wooden bases from scraps of wood, with dowels in the middle. On these bases, my mother put globs of paper mache. Then, she formed puppets using only her fingers, a nail file and matches, leaving a small extension at the neck of each puppet. This extension became the base to add clothing made from scraps of material. After the puppets were dried, she painted them with oil paint she still had from her art projects.

A puppet theater consisted of a king and queen, a prince and princess, a jester, hobo, crocodile and a few other characters. Farmers bought them for gifts for their children for a few eggs, a loaf of bread, a liter of milk or a pound of flour. Sometimes, we put on a puppet show in Grandma's backyard. The entrance fee was any kind of food.

One day, my mother carefully dug up some spring flowers in my grandparents' yard. She made sure the flowers still had their complete roots. She placed them on a tree stump and drew them. Later, she carefully replanted the flowers, making sure they continued to grow. She explained that houses and people and their belongings could easily be destroyed, but the land and what grows on it, would always survive. All her re-planted flowers survived. This ritual seemed to be a kind of therapy for her. The flower drawings were also traded for food.

In early 1946, my mother helped decorate a newly-established restaurant. She painted chairs, benches and wardrobes. Her pay was several lunches for both of us, as well as several bottles of wine and food from the restaurant's kitchen. In August 2010, I visited Germany with my grandson. I introduced him to old family friends and took him to churches and cemeteries where his ancestors were baptized and buried. One place we visited was the former restaurant, now occupied by the owner's son and his family. I was surprised and happy to see that all my mother's work had been preserved and taken care of.

Wardrobe painted by my mother in 1946

Elfriede E. Wilde

HUNGER
Germany 1945-1946

Hunger is a gray ghost. Given the right environment, he will stalk you day and night, reaching for you with bony fingers, gnawing at your innards, tearing them apart, eating your flesh inch by inch, feeding you with hopelessness.

He whispers in your ear, "Are you strong enough to survive?" He takes over your brain and consumes your thoughts. Hunger makes babies whimper because they are too weak to cry, and it makes their mothers cry because they have nothing to give their babies. Hunger makes one look old with hollow, sunken eyes, skin hanging from skeletal frames.

People will roam woods, fields and meadows for food. They will pick dandelions and nettles and weeds and keep secret the cove of mushrooms and strawberries found deep in the woods. Hunger makes people do terrible things. They will eat horses, dogs, cats, even rats, to stay alive. They will scavenge in the rubble and ruins of houses for anything edible, and some will kill for food to keep their children alive.

Some of the causes of hunger are famine, war and hate among people and nations. Hunger can take anyone, young and old alike, and it will make them believe that God has forsaken them forever.

My "Apple Hat" that still keeps me warm
Texarkana, TX, 2015

MY "APPLE HAT"

There was very little to eat in Germany during the fall and winter of 1945. Heating material and warm clothing were luxury items and nearly impossible to find. On a cold afternoon, I stood in a line of people in front of a grocery store, hoping to buy something, anything, with my meager ration card before everything was sold out. I started talking with a woman who stood in line next to me.

I admired the lovely white fur cap the woman was wearing. She told me that it was a gift from her husband. He gave it to her long before the war. He had not returned from the war; he was still missing. She struggled to raise their three children alone. She would have loved to have some fresh food for her children, something like apples, and she was willing to trade something for it, something like her fur cap.

After my grandparents lost everything during the air raid in September 1944, my grandmother moved to a small village near the town of Backnang. My grandparents owned a little house there, surrounded by a garden with fruit trees. Grandpa worked for the railroad and had to stay in Stuttgart. I knew Grandma still had a few apples in her cellar, stored in open wooden shelves.

A week later, I stood in front of the house where the woman with the three children lived, carrying a bucket full of Grandma's apples. We had exchanged addresses while standing in line at the grocery store. The house was badly damaged. I could tell the woman was embarrassed to be living like that. She brought the fur cap to the door and handed it to me. When I gave her the large bucket full of apples, she started to cry.

"Tears of joy," she said wiping her eyes, because now she had a Christmas gift for her children. She also could keep the bucket.

I put the cap on immediately. The fur was wonderfully warm, and the hat so very elegant. Most women only had old, worn head scarves left to keep them warm. I felt like a princess. I wore the hat for years nearly every day during the cold German winters.

In 1957, I immigrated to the United States of America. We have made many trips since then, my fur cap and I. We went to New York and Washington D.C. together as well as to the state of Washington. We traveled to Canada, to Alaska and to many other cold places.

I now live in Texas. Snow is a rarity here, but occasionally the temperature drops to thirty-two degrees or even a little below. These are the days when I take my "apple hat" from the closet, and old memories awaken. In the more than seventy years that I have owned the hat, it has been cleaned and relined several times, but people still admire it.

This is what happened here in the photo with Santa Claus on the Coca Cola throne in a local supermarket. I shopped early one morning, long before the children came to sit on Santa's lap to tell him what they wanted for Christmas and to have their picture taken with him. As I passed Santa, he asked where I found the beautiful hat. I stopped and told him and the few shoppers who had gathered around us the story of my apple hat. Santa insisted to have his photo taken with me, a woman in her eighties. Must have been because of the hat.

"A lovely story," said the people who heard it, smiling.

I am not sure that they believed me. Here, in a supermarket with shelves filled to the ceiling with all kinds of food one could think of, people could not believe or even imagine that, back then, people in Germany were starving and freezing. I will never forget the woman's tears of joy. We had made a good trade—a bucket full of apples for a fur cap that still keeps me warm today.

WILHELMSGLUECK

Wilhelmsglueck was a pediatric nursing school. It also was a home for young orphans and children whose parents were unable to care for them. Due to the destruction during the war, many parents still lived in bomb shelters or nearly uninhabitable ruins, unable to provide for their children.

The home and school belonged to the Lutheran Diakonissenanstalt, a very large hospital in a nearby town. It was supervised by deaconesses, sisters of the Lutheran church. They can be compared to nuns but wear different habits. Our training consisted of studying as well as hands-on training. We changed diapers, bathed the children and fed them, played with them and took complete care of them. During night shift, we boiled and cleaned the glass bottles that were used to feed the children. The rubber nipples had to be cleaned with salt, then also boiled to keep them sterile. Cloth diapers were soaked in tubs, boiled in big pots on wood-heated stoves and dried on outside clothes lines. It was hard, meticulous work, requiring strict discipline.

One day, a new child was admitted who came down with measles several days later. The fear of an epidemic created instant panic. Two doctors arrived from the big hospital. Since regular vaccinations were not available, every nursing student who had measles previously was asked to donate blood. Every child in the home was inoculated with our blood. This is called passive immunization. We had avoided an epidemic.

The school was situated on a farm that also belonged to the hospital. Most of the food the children, staff and students ate was raised directly on the farm. The farm had a big herd of cows supplying milk for the children. Food was still very scarce, and much of the produce and milk was sent to the hospital.

Our breakfast consisted of a watery cabbage soup and one-half slice of black bread. At 10:00 a.m., we had our first break and were served a small glass of buttermilk and red beets. When I first arrived at the school, the morning break was heaven, something to eat when I was hungry. Soon, though, the combination of buttermilk and red beets lost its fascination. The beets did not mix well with buttermilk, and I was unable to eat them anymore. I still drank my glass of buttermilk, but until this day I cannot stand the taste of red beets. Our Saturday evening meals were treats—three pretzels with a small piece of butter and a cup of coffee substitute made from barley malt.

Besides taking care of the children, we had classes, and we studied hard. On Sundays, we were supposed to attend a devotional service held by one of the sisters. None of us were happy about that service, and we tried extremely

hard to get out of it by volunteering to wash cloth diapers or help in the kitchen. Nightshift service the night before assured a long sleep-in on Sunday morning.

One warm summer day, one of the sisters announced that we all were attending a revival in a nearby church that evening. We were wondering what a revival was. None of us had ever heard about it, and none of us wanted to attend a church service. We would rather spend an hour or two of our limited free time doing something more pleasant. But we could not get out of it.

The walk to the village church took about fifteen minutes. People had already congregated outside the church, including several young men who, much to the dismay of the sisters, looked at us with interest. I do not believe that any of us heard or understood much of the service. The young men glanced at us, while we giggled behind our hands. We decided that revival was not too bad.

When the service was over, several of the young men asked if they could accompany us back to the school. The sisters did not know how to handle this situation in front of other people in the congregation. They walked silently behind us while we happily flirted with our escorts. Two more evenings of revival service followed, and we made plans with our new friends to meet again the next evening. Unfortunately, the sisters were not impressed with our sudden interest to attend church. Revival was cancelled.

After graduation, I accepted a position with a family who owned a trucking business. I took care of their young daughter who had scoliosis. I also did light housework and helped in the office.

THE PIG

Nobody knew where the pig came from. Karl, one of the truck drivers who had brought it, only said it came from a farm. Where else would a pig come from? It certainly was not wandering around in the big city. Maybe Karl had traded some of his wife's jewelry or some children's toys for it. His two children were teenagers now, too old to play with small toys. Farmers were willing to trade for such things. The year was 1948. People were still starving.

We all stared at the pig locked in a large wooden crate. Some of the men unloaded it quietly, unnoticed by the neighbors. They carried the crate into the garage and hid it amongst boxes of tools and machinery.

Now the question was how to butcher and dress the pig. This act was strictly illegal, and a person could go to jail for it. In fact, the farmer who sold the pig could go to prison also. Every farmer had to sell a certain amount of what he produced to the government. This included milk from his cows, eggs and produce. If an animal became too ill to recover, a veterinarian was called to perform an emergency slaughter of the animal. If the animal did not have a contagious decease, the farmer could keep a certain portion of the meat for himself and his family. The rest had to be turned over to the government to help feed a starving population.

Nobody knew how to butcher a pig. One of the men told us to heat large pots of water on the wood stove. Nobody knew why, but he said that farmers heated water when they butchered a pig. After much discussion, everyone thought the best way would be to shoot the animal.

Felix, one of the truck drivers, had a pistol. The weapon was not registered, but he carried it on his long trips to protect himself and his cargo. It would come in handy now to shoot a pig. But how would they keep the nosy neighbors from hearing the gun shot? The group decided that two of the drivers should go to the yard, start two of the trucks and keep them running for about ten minutes, drowning out the din of the shot. This diversion would give Felix enough time to shoot the pig. The pig had other ideas. As the men opened the door of the crate, the pig bolted out and jumped over a stack of tools. Frantically, the men chased the animal. The pig and the men nearly demolished the garage. Finally, they caught it.

The guys outside, not knowing what was going on in the garage, decided enough time had elapsed, and they shut off the engines. Three seconds later, the shot fell. For a moment, everyone was paralyzed with fear. I felt faint, my heart was beating rapidly. A window flew open in the house next door.

Mr. Kunz, dressed in a dirty T-shirt and unshaven, yelled, "What is going on down there?"

"One of the trucks backfired," Hans yelled back. "Sorry we disturbed you." With a bang the window closed.

Now everyone sprang into action. The pig was carried to the cellar. The dressing and preparing took place by the light of a few candle stubs and some flashlights.

That night, a great feast was held behind closed doors. There was pork roast, one or two small potatoes for everyone, and dandelion and nettle salad—and wine!

Even though people had little food, the grape harvest had been good and there was no shortage of wine.

NEW MONEY

Just a few months later, initiated by the United States Military Government, the German currency changed from the old RM (*Reichsmark*) to the new DM (*Deutsche Mark*). It happened on Sunday, June 20, 1948. Announcements were made the day before over the radio and by notices posted in strategic places around town. People were asked to go to the place where they picked up their monthly ration cards. In exchange for 60 RM, every person received 40 DM. One month later, everyone received an additional 20 DM. Bank accounts and savings devalued ten to one, but that money was not available for a while.

The next day, people, not believing that what they saw was true, stood in front of store windows that were filled overnight with items not available before, except through the black market. Now shelves were filled with food and other items, but money was scarce.

Some of our friends did not believe this would last. They immediately bought as much food as they could, spending nearly all their new money. However, the black market was ending, and Germany's new stable economy was beginning. Many items were now available without ration cards, but not everything. Butter was still rationed for a while, and sugar was rationed until 1950.

CHRISTMAS EVE IN RUSSIA

My father was never around as much as I would have liked when I grew up. In fact, he missed some of my most important years, changing from a little girl into a teen. When he was drafted into the German army in 1941, my parents were not together any more. Serving in a radio unit in Finland, he was captured by the Russians in 1945, shortly before the end of the war. We knew nothing of his fate for more than two years.

Then one day, my paternal grandmother received a postcard with a very brief message from him through the Red Cross. He was in a Russian prisoner-of-war camp, and he was well. Attached to the card was a return card with writing and mailing instructions. The message could not be more than twenty-five words.

A month later, I also received a card from him. He was allowed to send one card a month. In one of his cards, he asked if I could send him a recent photo of myself. The instructions stated that the photo had to be sewn to the card with needle and thread in such a manner that nothing could be put under it. In that case, only the name of the sender was allowed—no message.

My father was in the Russian prison camp from April

1945 to October 1949. When he returned home, he told us very little about his time there. Occasionally, he would share bits and pieces with me.

Since the Russians themselves were not showered with riches, conditions were deplorable. Food was not plentiful and not very good. The prisoners slept on wooden benches, covered only with their coats. They did not have enough room to sleep on their backs; so they crammed together sideways. After a while, they all woke up around the same time during the night and turned over. One night, my father could not turn over because the man next to him had died. People died in the barracks during the night; others froze to death while using the outside latrines.

My father told me that the one thing, the only thing, that helped him survive, was to bond with a few other prisoners. They had to work in the daytime, but in the evening, they enjoyed a short period of relaxation. He and his friends used this time to keep their minds active. They fashioned chess pieces from scraps of wood, and my father, a chess-champion, taught them to play chess. One man remembered many poems that he had learned in school. He recited them, and the others tried to memorize them. My father who spoke French fluently also taught them French. One man, a mathematical whiz, gave them math problems to solve. My father was convinced that these activities kept them alive.

One extremely cold winter, my father was assigned with other prisoners to cut down trees in a forest. When they were walking back to camp one evening, he stumbled and fell into the knee-deep snow. A guard told him to get up and keep going. The snow felt wonderful. All he wanted was to stay there, go to sleep and not feel tired any more. The guard told him again to get up and keep moving. My father ignored him. He did not feel the cold snow. He actually felt warm and at peace, and he wanted to stay there forever. The guard prodded him several times with his gun, then realizing that he would not or could not get up, the guard picked my father up, hoisted him over his shoulder and carried him back to camp. He saved my father's life.

Every time workers were needed for certain jobs, my father volunteered. He volunteered to build outside ovens for baking; he became a carpenter to help construct an addition to a building; and he became a baker, even though he had never worked in any of these jobs. One day, while working in the bakery, he was mixing bread dough. Hungry and near starvation, he ate some of the dough. His stomach revolted, and he immediately threw up the dough. He ate again what he threw up and this time was able to keep it down.

My father also started to learn, understand and then speak the Russian language by talking to any guard who was willing to speak with him. Languages came naturally to both my parents. Both spoke several languages. One day, help was needed in the medical office, mostly for keeping medical records. A female doctor ran the medical clinic. Due to his newly-acquired Russian language skills, my father received the job. Shortly after starting this new job, he discovered vitamins in bottles in a drawer. He stole a few pills and shared them with his closest friends, trying to improve his and their well-being. During the next few weeks, he stole vitamins again several times. One day, the doctor caught him in the act! He was convinced he would be executed. To his surprise, the lady doctor propositioned him, and he accepted. Again, his life was saved.

I forgot the exact time when the first trains arrived in Stuttgart after the war, carrying soldiers who had been prisoners-of-war. I also do not know how the news traveled that a train was arriving. Still, I remember the day when I watched prisoners disembark, rags hanging over skeleton bodies, some missing limbs, some supporting each other to walk. A few carried small cardboard boxes, tied with string, but most of them were empty-handed. People, mostly women, stood silently on the side. Many quietly held up photos of loved ones, hoping that one of the returning soldiers had some information for them. What I remember most is the silence—so many people and hardly a sound could be heard.

When my father was released from prison in October 1949, he wore his old army coat, a black fur cap, had swollen legs and hated cabbage. He refused to eat any dish that contained cabbage for the rest of his life.

After my father was home for two or three days, he announced that he had to go to downtown Stuttgart. He did not say why he had to go nor when he would be back. He left early in the morning and returned in late afternoon, unwilling, or maybe unable, to talk about where he had gone. Many weeks later he told me a story.

Shortly after my father had arrived in the prison camp in 1945, he met a young man, actually a boy not even eighteen years old, who had been drafted into the German army at the very end of the war. He was from Stuttgart, his parents' only child. He was happy when they finally were allowed to send postcards home and when he received two return cards from his parents. My father included him in his group of friends, and they sat together at the dinner table.

Most of the time dinner consisted of a watery cabbage soup and some bread. One evening, after a hard day of work, the young man looked at the soup with disgust and declared in a loud voice, "I will not eat this crap anymore."

One of the guards came over to inquire what was going on. The boy repeated his decision not to eat. Without success, the guard told him to eat, finally prodding him with his gun. The boy picked up his tin plate and threw the soup into the guard's face. In seconds, he was surrounded by several guards.

My father watched helplessly as they took the boy away. Nobody knew what happened to him. He never returned. That day, when my father went downtown, he had visited the boy's parents. They had received two postcards from their son, and then the mail had stopped. The Red Cross was unable to find out anything. Two years later, they finally heard from my father what had happened to their son. My father told me that it was one of the hardest things he ever had to do, and then he never mentioned it again.

My father was in the prison camp nearly three years when rumors started circulating that the men would be released and taken back to Germany soon. One evening, the rumors came true. Officials came to their barracks and read a list of names, telling the men to pack their meager belongings and line up outside the building early the next morning. They were going home!

The men exchanged addresses with those staying behind, promising to visit their families and bring them information about their loved ones. Addresses had to be memorized, not even one handwritten scrap of paper could be taken. The next morning, the men lined up outside the building. Trucks arrived to take them to the train station. The men climbed on the trucks as their names were called.

At the end, there were a few dozen men whose names had not been called. They had to return to the barracks. The trucks drove to the train station. Again, the men lined up and got on the train when their names were called, and again several dozen men were left behind. Once on the train, there was another roll call. Those whose names were not called had to leave the train and were taken back to the barracks. My father made it on the train one time, then had to go back. He was unable to describe the emotional punishment when he told me about it. When he finally was released, he did not believe it until his train had crossed the border, and he arrived in Friedland, a transit camp for German soldiers released from Russian prisons.

My father also told me about one Christmas Eve in Russia. It was one of several Christmas Eves he spent in prison, but to him, it was the most meaningful and the most beautiful Christmas Eve in his whole life. The men in camp were working in the forest cutting down trees during that long, cold, harsh winter. As Christmas approached, they noticed that their already meager bread rations had become even smaller. Of course, this did not help raise their spirits.

The Russians do not celebrate Christmas like the German people do, but they knew about the German custom of celebrating Christmas Eve. On that day, they brought the prisoners back to camp early in the afternoon. The men were grateful to get out of the bitter cold, but as they sat in their barracks, morale was at its lowest.

As evening came, some laid down on the wooden benches that served as their beds. Others huddled together in small groups and talked in low voices about home and Christmas Eves long past. They had not heard from their families since the war ended, and they did not know if their loved ones were still alive. Communication by mail was still forbidden. A few just sat and stared into space, and all were hungry.

One man dug into his pockets and brought out a small candle and some matches. Nobody knew how he had gotten them. Carefully, he placed the candle in a tin plate and lit it. Some of the others gathered around and tried desperately to get a Christmas carol started, but no one felt like singing.

Suddenly, the door opened and several Russian Guards entered the room. They carried stretchers covered with towels. They set them down in the middle of the room and removed the towels. The men looked up in surprise, and then they just stared. They could not believe what they saw.

The stretchers were loaded with loaves and loaves of freshly baked bread. They saw the bread, could smell it, and yet they still did not believe it. The guards passed out the bread, one big loaf for every man. They held it in their hands, just looking at it. Some laughed; some cried. And then the big room grew silent as each man took a bite from his own loaf of bread.

Many years later, my father told me that at that moment he would not have traded places with any king in the world, for what greater gift could anyone receive than those hungry, starving men did on that Christmas Eve. They even forgot the shortened rations during the past weeks, because only in this way was their gift of bread made possible.

Later, with all stomachs filled and the terrible hunger pains stilled, the men gathered around the little candle which burned brightly on the tin plate. Someone started to sing *Stille Nacht, Heilige Nacht* (Silent Night, Holy Night), and they all joined in. All bitterness had left their hearts. For the first time in many months, the men had hope again, hope that one day they would go home and be reunited with their families, hope that a future life was still waiting for them thousands of miles away. They remembered the words "good will toward men," and they felt the Christmas spirit in their hearts.

Elfriede E. Wilde

SCOTLAND

My father and I were sitting in the waiting room at the Stuttgart-Echterdingen Airport. It was June 1, 1950, and I was about to board a Pan-American flight to England. Since this flight was my first one, I was excited and a little nervous.

When my father returned from Russia, he was fortunate to be reinstated in his old job at his former place of work. Pre-war business connections were re-established, and companies slowly started to emerge from the destruction of the war. A former business friend from Edinburgh, Scotland, visited the company my father worked for. He was looking for a business translator and for someone who could help occasionally with their young child. Since I had a pediatric nursing degree and spoke English, I immediately applied for the position, was accepted and signed a two-year contract.

The Echterdingen airport opened in early 1939, but in fall of the same year, it was closed for civilian traffic and taken over by the German Air Force. From 1945 until 1948, the American Air Force used the airfields. Sometime in 1948, the first civilian flights started again. The planes were propeller-powered; no civilian jet planes existed yet. In November 2013, the name of the airport changed to Manfred Rommel Airport in honor of the former mayor of Stuttgart, son of General Erwin Rommel, the Desert Fox.

Traveling by airplane in 1950 was still something rare and special. My father made sure I was dressed appropriately. He had a gray travel costume made for me by an excellent tailor, then went shopping with me for a matching hat, gloves and shoes. I had insisted that my father be the only person to see me off. We only had eight months together since his release from the Russian prisoner-of-war camp, and I treasured these last minutes with him.

I boarded the Pan-American flight at 1:30 p.m. I changed planes in London and arrived in Edinburgh at 9:00 p.m. The family in Scotland received me with open arms and immediately made me part of their family. Mr. and Mrs. Smith were both Oxford-educated. With their help, my school English improved rapidly. Between doing translations for their printing firm and helping with Roger, their three-year-old son, I still had lots of free time to explore the city and travel around the country.

I had to adjust to driving on the left side of the road, to round doorknobs, to flushing commodes by pulling strings attached to tanks at the ceiling, and to conquering other difficulties. I soon fell in love with the city and its history. I visited the castle, walked on Princes Street and enjoyed the Princes Street Gardens with its flower clock. I even climbed Arthur's Seat, one of the earliest known sites of human habitation in the area.

In 1951, the Edinburgh Zoo started its weekly Penguin Parade. Little Roger and I made many visits to watch what is today a big tourist attraction. Sometimes, we were the only spectators, and we had a great time. I also walked from the castle down the Royal Mile to Holyrood Palace where Mary, Queen of Scots, resided. In February of 1952, I listened to an announcement from a pulpit in this street, made by a man who wore a black robe and a powdered wig.

"The King is dead! Long live the Queen!" King George VI had died.

Someone told me about a German church in the area. I really was not interested in going to a church, any church, and I was glad that the family I lived with were also not church-going people. Still, I thought I might meet some other Germans there, and I did. Like me, most of them only came to socialize.

Soon, I belonged to a group who took bicycle tours around the area. We bicycled all over Scotland. Once we went on a two-week tour through the Highlands. We visited Loch Ness, hoping to see the monster. We bicycled to Ft. Williams and took boats to Loch Linhee and Loch Etive. We went camping at Aberdour, pitching our tents on the silver sand beach, diving into the ocean for early morning swims. We visited Melrose Abbey, bicycled North to Inverness and saw many of the old Scottish castles. The summer days were long and beautiful. Daylight lasted until after ten o'clock at night. It was a great time to be alive.

During my second week in Edinburgh, I went to a nearby produce shop to buy some fruits. The proprietors were friends of the Smith family. I remember looking at watermelons, a fruit that I had never seen nor tasted before. There were three other customers in the store. Suddenly, one of them let out a terrifying scream.

"A mouse, a mouse!" she yelled. Within seconds, she jumped on a chair, frantically clutching her skirt around her. The two other women, also screaming, climbed on a bench.

Looking around, I saw the little mouse behind a wooden crate, looking just as scared as the women. I bent down and gently grabbed the little frightened creature by its tail, took it outside and released it by the side of the road.

When I came home with my purchases, Mrs. Smith had already received a call from her friend at the store, who apparently told her the story in comical details.

"Elisabeth," Mrs. Smith said, "please don't do anything like this again. A proper lady does not catch mice in a store."

"What should I have done?" I asked, aghast at the thought of having committed a faux pas.

"You should have also screamed and jumped up on a chair or bench."

The mouse never reappeared in the store, and I never had a chance to act like a proper English lady.

I also made many new Scottish friends. I learned some of the Scottish Highland dances and went to the Highland Festivals at the Castle. Several times a year, we went to Elie, a small coastal town in Fife. The Smith family had a house directly on the beach. I had never seen the ocean, and soon I was swimming every day, enjoying the waves and the golden sand on the beach. I met another German girl, Gerda, who was working in a nearby home. Together, we explored the area, the lighthouse, visited the Shell House at Leven and took afternoon trips to nearby St. Andrews for high tea.

The two years passed in a flash. Twin girls joined the family. I was asked to stay indefinitely if I wanted. I had a hard time saying good-bye; however, I was ready for new adventures and wanted to return to the continent.

THE SWITHBOARD GIRLS FROM *BURGHOLZHOF* (ROBINSON BARRACKS)

In 1946, the American Signal Section, part of the American Military Forces in Stuttgart, Germany, hired the first German female switchboard operators. The switchboard was located in the *Koenigsbau* on Koenigstrasse (King Street) and was called "Stuttgart Switch." My friend Annemarie worked for the German railroad during the war as a telephone operator. Someone told her that the Americans were hiring German women with a good command of the English language as telephone operators in the *Koenigsbau*. She applied for a position and was hired.

One very important aspect of the job was that the German employees received a free lunch every day. That lunch was worth more than money at that time. Germans were starving. Everything was still rationed, and people had to wait in long lines in front of stores to get a few groceries. Very often when they reached the front of the line, everything was sold out. I remember well that, in the summer of 1946, one could hardly find a potato in the city. Annemarie was happy to have this job. Every day at lunch, everyone received a slice of white bread. Annemarie took it home to her mother who made bread dumplings with it on weekends.

In 1950, the switchboard was moved to Robinson Barracks at the *Burgholzhof*. The first switchboard was in building 6. After working in Scotland for two years, I returned to Stuttgart in July 1952. I was unable to find work in the field for which I had a degree, but because of my knowledge of the English language, I was hired by the American Signal Section. In March 1953, we moved to building 129, which had just been completed. It housed the teletype section on the first floor. The switchboard was located on the second floor. Both belonged to the 589th Signal Section.

We were a group of forty-six girls who worked there. Our working relations with the Americans were excellent. On American holidays, soldiers brought plates of food from the mess hall. They brought turkey and dressing, vegetable plates with all sorts of vegetables we had never seen, salads, lemon pies, oranges, nuts and real coffee. These were delicacies that we had never heard of or had long forgotten.

Sometimes, we were invited to the American snack bar. There, we were introduced to hamburgers and cherry cokes, none of which we had ever tasted before. Once a week, we could eat for little money in the NCO club. The American women sold chili and homemade baked goods. The money was donated to several welfare organizations.

We found out that women were not so different, whether they were from Stuttgart, New York or Chicago. Many friendships formed. I was in close touch with two American friends for about fifty-five years—Dolly from Pittsburgh, Pennsylvania, and Ruth from Whitney, Texas. Ruth tried to teach me American cooking, without much success. It failed mostly because I could not find the ingredients in German stores. Dolly had more luck teaching me how to roll up my hair with bobby pins to make small curls all over my head. I loved that hairstyle. For my birthday, they gave me an American lipstick and the James A. Michener book *Fires of Spring*. Thus, my love affair with James Michener started. Today, I have read and now own most of his books.

Later, when I moved to the States with my husband, we still visited back and forth. Ruth and I lived near each other for a while at Ft. Hood in Texas, and I also met her family. Her mother taught me real Texan cooking. In turn, I showed her how to make a Swabian potato salad and *Spaetzle*, a small dumpling served in the Stuttgart area. Ruth and Dolly both died recently, and I miss them.

We worked eight hours each day for four days, then a sixteen-hour night shift every fifth night. In summer, we often went directly after the nightshift to the Bad Berg Pool to swim in the mineral water. The mineral water was cool, flowing swiftly, and was pleasant for swimming. The mineral springs in Stuttgart are the second largest in Europe after the springs in Budapest, Hungary.

During my years in Robinson Barracks, we were often invited to American celebrations. The soldiers taught us how to dance the jitterbug, and we tried, with much laughter, to teach them how to dance a real Vienna waltz, albeit with little success. Jitterbug and swing dancing were more their style. But they always treated us with courtesy and respect.

For most of us, the years after the war were still very difficult. Several of my colleagues were refugees from the Eastern parts of Europe. We still lived in temporary housing in bombed buildings, in barracks or in unheated attic rooms. To find a nice place to live was nearly impossible. We helped each other as much as we could. We borrowed each other's dresses so that we did not have to wear the same one every day, especially if we were invited to a dance. I wonder if these young soldiers realized that they brought sunshine into our still war-torn souls. Of course, permanent relationships formed. Over half of my colleagues, myself included, married American soldiers and followed them to America. My husband's ancestor came from Lomersheim, near Stuttgart, and immigrated to America in 1818.

Most of us are still in contact with each other today. The hardships of the war and the years immediately afterward bonded us together forever. Today, we are grandmothers and great-grandmothers scattered around the world, but we have not forgotten those years. Our American colleagues, male and female, are as much a part of Stuttgart's history as we are. We always had good working relationships with each other, and we never forgot these relationships.

Our group is small now. Whenever I visit Stuttgart, we

get together and reminisce about the 1950s, our youth and things that happened back then. When we tell our children and grandchildren how we appreciated little things, what a treat a chocolate bar, a piece of pie or a cup of real coffee was, they do not understand. This makes us sad, because as hard as that time was, it still enhanced and formed our lives.

JAMES

He left beautiful memories and a tiny lingering sadness for days that are gone forever. He drove away shadows that still haunted me after the war, and he gave me sunshine days. He made me laugh and see things that I had forgotten or could not see anymore, like squirrels chasing each other around trees in the park or a lizard sunning himself on the rocks of a bombed-out house. One day, while walking in the park, we were caught in an unexpected rainstorm. James grabbed my hand, and we ran around the lake, splashing through the puddles, laughing and giggling, then raced up the steps to the opera house, seeking shelter between the huge pillars that held up the roof.

Grinning, he looked at me and said, "You look a mess."

The rainbow that followed the cloud burst was spectacular. James was still holding my hand.

I had passed this young, handsome man with black, curly hair and sparkling dark eyes several times in the hall of the building where we both worked. He had just transferred from another part of Germany to work in the Signal section where I also was employed. He always smiled pleasantly and said "good morning" when we met going to work and "good night" when we left in the evening. He never yelled "Hey gorgeous, what are you doing tonight?", a common GI come-on.

One day he stopped me. "Excuse me miss. May I ask you a question?" The other girls had told him that I knew more about the history of our town than anyone else. Was this true, he wanted to know.

My grandpa, a history buff, loved our town. Ever since I could remember, he told me about Stuttgart's history, how the city started in the thirteenth century and how it grew to become the metropolis of today. We went to the Volksfest together, the big festival held every fall along the meadows of the Neckar River. This festival started in 1818 as an agricultural festival. A fruit column is erected each year, decorated with fruits and vegetables. Today, the Volksfest is known for its beer tents and music festivals. There are carnival rides, animals and booths offering food and merchandise. I always loved the Volksfest.

Grandpa also took me to the circus and to museums with dinosaurs and Indians. We visited the Stiftskirche, the big cathedral where one of our ancestors, Matthaeus Alber the Reformer, preached in the sixteenth century and where he married his daughter to Felix Gaspar in 1561. We climbed the steps to the castle where our other ancestors had lived and reigned for centuries. Grandpa instilled a love for reading and history in me, a love that stayed with me throughout my life. He grieved about the city's nearly complete destruction by bombs during the war. It took years and years to rebuild. He did not live long enough to see the rebirth of his beloved town.

Yes, I knew the story of my town, a town that was still showing the scars of war.

"Would you tell me about it and maybe show me around the town one day?" James asked.

For a moment, I was speechless. An American soldier was interested in the history of a town that was destroyed by American bombs not so long ago? I thought GIs were only interested in German beer and German girls. The first thing most of them did as soon as they arrived in Germany was to buy a car to impress the girls. Most Germans could not afford a car, not even a small one. They walked, and if they were fortunate, they rode bicycles or motor scooters. Others rode streetcars and trains when they were running again. We all gawked at the huge American automobiles. To us, they were a sign of unbelievable riches.

"Oh yes, I would be happy to show you my town," I said.

James looked a little wistful and said, "I don't have a car. I am saving for college."

I laughed. I was going to like this man. "A car would be a hindrance. To show you around, we will have to walk or take a streetcar."

He smiled. "When do you have time?"

"How about this evening after work?" I hoped that he did not think me too forward to suggest a meeting so soon. I told him to meet me at dusk in front of the main lobby at the train station.

"Why at the train station?" he wanted to know. "We are not going on a train ride, or are we?"

"No," I said, "but I have a special treat for you."

My grandfather worked for the railroad, and often he had taken me up to the very top of the tower at the train station. I loved watching the trains from up there. They were coming into and leaving the station continuously. The ten-story high tower also gave a spectacular view of the city below, the city I was born in and loved so much.

James was already waiting when I stepped off the streetcar in front of the station. We walked through the huge, crowded lobby to the tower entrance and took the elevator to the observation platform. As we stepped off the elevator and walked through the door out to the platform, I could hear James catching his breath. The sky was darkening, and the city lights below had come on. It is an unforgettable sight.

We went over to the railing that encircled the platform. The hills, with their twinkling lights, wound themselves around the town like a diamond necklace. We were quiet for a while. Then James asked why dark spots lay between the lights. I explained that these were bombed-out buildings. The city had many scars. It would take many years to rebuild. I pointed out some of the illuminated landmarks, the *Hindenburgbau* directly below us, the *Tagblatt Turm* to the south, *Koenigstrasse* (King Street) going southwest from the train station to the castle square. We could see the Old Castle, but there were no lights in the ruins of the New Castle. There was still much darkness to the west, the part of town where I grew up. It was nearly all destroyed.

"What was it like before the war, when you were a child?" James asked.

I told him about my grandpa, the faraway places the trains came from and the magic of the city lights with no dark spots in between. This place was my fairytale land, and I was the princess in the tower.

The tower was built in 1922 about the time the new railroad station was built. Even though the train station was destroyed in the war, the tower miraculously remained standing. In 1952, an illuminated rotating Mercedes star was added to the very top. The star is one of Stuttgart's famous landmarks.

We realized that we both worked night shift the next day. After that day, we tried to arrange our night shifts together as often as possible. James made coffee in the break room, real coffee, not the substitute coffee made from barley malt that we usually drank. He generously shared it with the other girls who also happened to work on these nights.

During the slow hours, we sat together sipping coffee, and James opened up this land called America for me with the same fierce pride and love that I felt about my hometown. He told me about its government and how it worked, how a president was elected, about the freedom that people had, about how they could vote for anyone they wanted and how they could make their opinions known. He vividly described the beginnings of the country, the Revolutionary War, the hardships of the early settlers. I learned about the California Gold Rush, the Civil War between the States, and about how the country is united now and called the United States of America. He described how the stores were loaded with food and how nearly everyone had a car, a radio and a telephone.

I never dreamed that such a place existed. It sounded like paradise. Even though ration cards were eliminated in May 1950, many people were still hungry and lacked daily necessities. The German people had lost everything, and it would take a long time for a destroyed country and its people to recover.

James was an ambitious young man. He had finished college, then was drafted into the army. After fulfilling his obligation to his country, he planned to go to law school. He was saving money for this venture. He was very passionate about it and shared his dreams for the future with me. He was also planning to be rich one day.

For weeks and months, we spent evenings, weekends or the days after night shifts to explore the city. My English was still not always adequate, but James's tutoring helped me improve greatly. I loved introducing him to the history of my town, and in the process, rediscovered nearly forgotten treasures that Grandpa had showed me.

One day, we stood before the ruins of the Kleines Haus, one of the opera houses. It was built around 1910 and burned in 1944. Before the war, opera, ballet and theater were important parts of our culture, and they are still today. I remembered the fairytale performances that I had seen here as a child with my mother. Every year, just before Christmas, my mother invited several of my friends and took us to the theater to see fairytales like *Hansel and Gretel*, *Cinderella*, *Sleeping Beauty* and *Puss'n Boots*. Looking at what was once a beautiful building, childhood memories washed over me, and I started to weep. I could not help it. James stood helplessly by. He did not say a word; he just took my hand in his. Later, I wondered how he had felt standing next to a weeping girl, knowing her pain was caused by actions of his fellow men. Still, it was comforting to have him standing next to me.

The theater was rebuilt and opened for performances again in 1962, but not in the old style. Some people said that the modern building looks interesting. I never liked it. Even today, I still think it looks ugly.

James's grandparents were poor immigrants from Europe. Their country also suffered much destruction, some at the hand of Germans. We never felt any bitterness about the war and the things that happened, only sadness. We were two young people, enjoying each other's company in a still beautiful city that was rising again from the ashes. Life abounded all around us. It was a good time to be alive. The scars of the past were still there, but they were fading.

Many of the old historical buildings still lay in ruins, but rebuilding had begun. There was City Hall whose history dated back to 1456, when the first building was erected by Count Ulrich of Wuerttemberg, one of my ancestors. Over the centuries, there were several buildings serving as City Hall.

In 1905, a new City Hall was dedicated, and a bell tower was added in 1925. Each side of the tower had a large clock, and bells played songs at certain times. In September 1944, City Hall, like nearly all of the inner city, was destroyed by bombs and fire. The building was not reconstructed in its old form. Only the bell tower and part of a sidewall were left standing as witnesses to the once beautiful, old architecture. Unfortunately, someone decided to recreate City Hall in a modern style, but the bells still play folk songs, bringing back old memories. In the square in front of City Hall is a fountain. James and I often stopped there for a drink. A new City Hall was dedicated in 1956, long after James had left.

The New Castle also still lay in ruins. Only part of the outer walls remained with gaping holes where windows used to be. It was built as a Baroque residence by Duke Carl Eugene and was completed in 1793. On one side of the castle was the Rose Garden. The garden was open again for the public, but still in a state of disarray. In front of the castle is the *Schlossplatz*, the castle square, where two of my friends and I sought shelter from the firestorm on September 12, 1944. Today, the reconstructed castle shines in its old glory. The Rose Garden is a place of joy and beauty again.

Immediately south of the *Schlossplatz* is the *Alte Schloss*, the Old Castle, where my ancestors reigned for centuries. The area was called *Stutengarden*, a breeding place for horses, and the name eventually evolved to Stuttgart. The Coat of Arms for the city still is a galloping black horse on a yellow background. Old documents show that Duke Liutolf, a son of Emperor Otto the Great, raised horses in that area in 949. Liutolf built a small castle, surrounded by a moat, to keep out intruders and to keep his horses safe. Later, a fortress replaced the small castle. In 1553, Count Christoph started to remodel the fortress. He added new interiors, transforming it from a fortress into a castle.

When James and I visited the Old Castle, part of it was open to the public again. Again, I was impressed by James' historical knowledge. One of the exhibits showed weapons and crosses from the time of the crusade, and he knew more about it than I did. We had great discussion about that time in history. Many years later, I discovered that I have crusade ancestors who lived in Jerusalem for years. We also visited the exhibits of the former queens' and princesses' gowns and, of course, the fantastic crown jewels.

One of the castle's unique features is the *Reitertreppe*, an inside stairway built for horses and their riders. The broad steps made it possible for riders to ride to the upper floor directly to the *Rittersaal*, the Knights' Hall. Like nearly all of the castle, this part was also destroyed in 1944. Reconstruction of the castle started as early as 1946; and even though it was not completed until about 1962, it still was a beautiful place to visit.

The *Reitertreppe* was already completed. In the courtyard stood the statue of Count Eberhard the Bearded, also one of my ancestors. When the castle burned all around it, the statue was untouched by the fire. Only the base was damaged and had to be replaced. In 1948, the Wuerttemberg State Museum was housed in the castle with its many historical exhibits dating back to Roman times. There was so much to see inside the castle. It was a great place to visit on rainy days.

On the other side of the castle, far away from its main entrance, is a crescent-shaped stone fountain. It can be seen from the castle gardens and the *Schlossplatz*, the Castle Square.

One day, as we were sitting on one of the iron benches in the *Schlossplatz,* James asked, "Why are we never going to the fountain?"

He had noticed that I always carefully guided him around and away from the fountain when we visited the castle or went to the market square. Tears came to my eyes.

"James," I pleaded, "I cannot go there."

I told him the story of the horror night of September 1944 when three young, terrified girls were fleeing through the burning city, climbing over tons of rubble and around dead bodies, hoping to find safety in the castle square. I told him of the wounded, the dying and the dead on the trampled grass that was now such a beautiful place again, and, trembling, I told him of the blood in the well.

Suddenly, I noticed James was holding me tight, wiping away my tears with his handkerchief. He kissed me gently on the forehead.

"We won't go to the fountain," he assured me. "You will know when the time is right and you are ready." He never mentioned the fountain again. We continued to take the streets that bypassed it.

After I moved to the United States, I visited my hometown occasionally. Like earlier years, I loved to walk through the city, through the parks, visiting the old historical sites. Sometimes, I searched in vain for landmarks that had disappeared during the rebuilding of the city. On a bright, sunny afternoon in June 1977, I stood across the road from the fountain, separated by a busy street. Cars and trucks whizzed by, streetcars stopped to load and unload passengers. Crowds of people milled around me. I turned to leave. I still could not bring myself to go to the fountain. Suddenly, I had the strangest feeling that someone was putting an arm around my waist.

A nearly forgotten, but still very familiar voice said, "The time is right. I know you can do it. Go drink from the fountain; it will bring healing."

I looked around and saw nobody there, only strangers rushing by. When the next walking light flashed, I joined the crowd to cross the street. Slowly I walked to the fountain. Nobody paid any attention to me. I stood alone by the well and looked at the crystal-clear water in the basin. For just an instant, it appeared blood red. Then, just as quickly, it cleared.

"Thank you, James," I whispered. Then I cupped my hands under the running water from the fountain and took a long drink.

The *Schlossplatz* is the beautiful square in the center of the town. It is bordered by the New Castle, the Old Castle, the *Koenigsbau*, and the *Kunstgebaeude* (art building) with its gilded stag on top. The *Kunstgebaeude* was erected in 1913. The golden stag was installed by my girlfriend's great-great-grandfather. The building was destroyed in 1944, but the stag had been removed earlier and put in an underground shelter. Today, it sits atop the dome again, after reconstruction of the building was completed in 1961.

In the middle of the square is the thirty-meter-high *Jubilaeumssaeule*, an anniversary column. The top is crowned with a sculpture of the goddess Concordia, representing unity. The column was erected in 1841 to commemorate the twenty-five-year reign of King Wilhelm I. In the midst of the destruction, it was left standing.

On Sunday mornings, we sometimes went to the *Schlossplatz* to listen to concerts in the pavilion. These concerts had recently started again. Right behind the pavilion and exactly across the square from the New Castle is the *Koenigsbau*, the King's Building. In earlier times, the king held parties and festivals there. It housed the stock exchange and the most elegant stores in the city before the war. It was a grand building with thirty-four columns along the front. In summer, a person could sit under the columns and be served coffee, pastries and drinks. Like other buildings along *Koenigstrasse*, it still lay in ruins. It was finally rebuilt in 1959 after I had left Germany and moved to America.

Today, the columns of the *Koenigsbau* are rebuilt, and open-air cafes invite people to sit, look across the square, and admire the beautiful gardens. *Koenigstrasse*, the main street with elegant shops, is a pedestrian zone now and a shoppers' paradise.

After one Sunday concert, we walked over to the *Stiftskirche*, the big cathedral with its two different-looking towers. Due to financial problems at the beginning of the reformation, the west tower's top was never completed. While the south tower has a high steeple, the west tower was covered with a flat roof that was never changed. The church's roots go back centuries. Historians presumed that a building for worship stood here in the tenth century. The earliest documentation described a church in 1175, the church "To the Holy Cross." Over the centuries, additions were made to the building, and the name was changed to *Stiftskirche*.

I wanted to be sure that the morning service was over. I had no desire to sit and listen to a preacher. James never mentioned that he wanted to attend a church service. I presumed that he felt the same way as I did. Still, I had ties to this church through my ancestor Matthaeus Alber, a prominent Lutheran minister and reformer who preached there in the sixteenth century. For me, they were historical ties, not spiritual ties.

The church was destroyed by bombs in 1944. Only the two towers and part of the north wall remained. Many valuable art treasures were lost. Parts of the Golden *Kanzel* (the Golden Pulpit) were found in the ruins and later carefully restored. The lower part of the south tower dates back to the twelfth century. It survived the bombings in the war and is the oldest documented construction in Stuttgart. Some stones rescued from the rubble were used when the church was rebuilt. Even though the church was not fully restored yet, it was beautiful. Eventually the outside was reconstructed as it was before, but the inside was modernized to cater to congregations of today.

Stuttgart has many beautiful churches. Many were destroyed in the war; many were damaged. Not all were rebuilt in the early 1950s, and some were never rebuilt. We loved visiting churches to admire the architecture, the stained-glass windows, the paintings, the stone sculptures, the icons and the glowing candles. Sometimes there was beautiful music. This music was all I needed. I did not need the preaching of sermons. But I did feel a peace in these places, a peace I did not feel anywhere else. I never questioned why. I did not know how James felt about it because we never talked about it. The churches were just beautiful buildings to be admired. James told me that only very large cities had cathedral churches in America, and he did not think any of them were as beautiful as the ones he saw here.

I loved St. Markus Church. It was one of the few buildings in the area that was damaged but not completely destroyed by bombs. Services were held again in 1945. My grandparents were married in this church on April 5, 1913, by Pastor Gustav Gerok. I have their wedding Bible. It survived the war because they took it to the country together with a few other belongings, before the heavy bombings started. I also have their wedding picture, taken in St. Markus Church. Grandpa was wearing a black tuxedo and black top hat, Grandma a black wedding gown with lace and a white veil. This was the custom at that time, brides wore black dresses and white veils. The church was dedicated by the King and Queen of Wuerttemberg on April 12, 1908.

St. Eberhard Church on *Koenigstrasse* is a Catholic church built in 1808. Like much of *Koenigstrasse,* the church was destroyed in 1944. Reconstruction had just begun, and we could follow some of the rebuilding.

Johannes Church held many childhood memories for me. The church was completed in 1876. Part of it sits on an island of the *Feuersee* (fire lake), the other part at the entrance to the once very elegant *Johannesstrasse* (Johannes Street). The *Feuersee* is a lake whose water was used for fighting fires in the earlier days of the city. In wintertime, it was a skating paradise for children and adults alike. The church received very heavy damage during the September 1944 bombing. Some of my friends lived near the church, and some died that night. The church was rebuilt after the war with the outside reconstructed as it was before. The inside is completely different now. The destroyed tower was rebuilt without a steeple, in memory of the war destruction.

Just around the corner from the Old Castle is the *Schillerplatz*. The square is named for Friedrich von Schiller, the poet, also one of my ancestors. His statue, erected in 1839, stands in the middle of the square. It was removed and stored in a safe place just before bombs destroyed the area. It was brought back in 1945 shortly after the war ended. Before the war, the *Schillerplatz* with its cobblestones, framed by century-old buildings, was often described as one of the most beautiful squares in the world. Today, an outdoor flower market is held in the square twice a week.

In the southwest corner of the *Schillerplatz* is the *Fruchtkasten*. In the early days of the town, farmers had to bring the tenth of their harvest and produce to give to the king. Some of the harvest was stored here in case a catastrophe befell the city, like a fire or famine. When World War II caused both of these catastrophes, the *Fruchtkasten* had long ceased its original purpose. The building was restored in 1956, and today, as part of the Wuerttemberg State Museum, it houses a fine collection of musical instruments.

Directly behind the Old Castle to the west is the *Markthalle*, the market hall. It is a beautiful two-story building with arcades along the front. It was built in 1914, mostly for farmers to bring their produce to town in the early morning hours. Shopkeepers came early to pick the freshest produce for their customers. The *Markthalle* received very heavy damage in 1944, but only days after the bombing, small stands appeared under the scorched arcades. People offered whatever wares they still had.

Today, the place offers fresh produce, meats, fish, spices, flowers, cheeses and exotic fruits from around the world. The smells are tantalizing, and the restaurants offer the finest foods again. When I visited with James, it brought back memories of standing in line to buy horse meat during the war. Horse meat could be bought for half the ration allowed on a ration card. We strolled between the stands. I introduced James to gooseberries and red currants. He did not like either one very well. He did enjoy the red currant and streusel pie served with coffee in one of the newly opened restaurants.

James loved movies. He took me to several American movies, and one time we went to a German movie. Even though he could not completely follow the plot, he had a great time. He talked about the actors, their gestures and acting abilities, the costumes, the colors, the music and most of all the special effects. He was interested in everything that went into movie making.

James had impeccable manners and a flair for elegance.

"Which is the finest restaurant in town?" he asked one day.

That, of course, was the Park Hotel. I thought it must be equal to the *Waldorf-Astoria* I had heard about. I remembered my father before the war, wearing a tuxedo, and my mother looking stunning in a red silk dress with silver trim that complemented her black hair. They were getting ready to attend a ball at the Park Hotel.

Red was my mother's favorite color, but not my father's. He thought it was too "glitzy." However, his opinion did not diminish my mother's joy in wearing clothes that he did not always approve of. I remembered the faint scent of her Chanel perfume when she kissed me goodnight. They went to the Park Hotel for dinners frequently, and once or twice I was allowed to accompany them for a luncheon. The hotel was built in the early 1900s and always had the reputation as the finest restaurant and hotel in the city. In fact, it was the finest in the whole area. It was destroyed in 1944. Then it was rebuilt, even more elegant than before, and eventually catered to an elite group of people again.

"I wish I could take you to this place," James mused.

We went to the American snack bar or to the club sometimes. He introduced me to hamburgers, French fries, cherry cokes and doughnuts; and I was perfectly happy with these delicacies. After years of starvation, these were extra special treats. In turn, I took him to a small restaurant near the market square to sample *maultaschen*. The place had just opened and served this Swabian delicacy of meat and spinach-filled bread pockets. James loved it.

"The Park Hotel is very elegant and also very expensive," I told him.

James had some nice civilian clothes, a couple of slacks and sport shirts. He never wore his army uniform on our town excursions. Having lost everything in the war, my own wardrobe was slim. I only had four outfits for work. None of them would have been appropriate for such an exclusive hotel and restaurant.

"We could pool our money, and I could borrow a dress from my girlfriend," I suggested. "How about you? Does anyone in your unit have a dark suit you could borrow?"

At first, James firmly rejected the idea of pooling our money. If he could not pay for it, we would not go. We spent little money on our jaunts through town. There was an occasional streetcar fare, sometimes coffee at an outdoor café or a movie. Most museums and art galleries did not charge an entry fee at that time. Sightseeing was free.

After much persuasion and pointing out the changes in time compared to the customs of our parents, he reluctantly agreed to a date at the Park Hotel. He took care of the reservations. When I mentioned that one could not walk up to the Park Hotel on foot, nor get off the streetcar that stopped near the hotel, we made a plan.

The next Saturday evening, we met inside the train station in front of one of the gates. Walking over to the taxi stand, we pretended to have just come in on a train for an evening on the town. James looked dashing in a borrowed black suit. I wore a green satin dress, which he said complemented my auburn hair. The dress belonged to my friend Margit. She sometimes let me borrow her clothes. Her mother, a master seamstress and tailor, could create the most beautiful dresses from scraps. Margit was always dressed beautifully.

I also wore my mother's pearl necklace and antique aquamarine ring. My father had given them to her, but she was too superstitious to wear them. She said that pearls and aquamarine stones bring tears. She wanted to trade them to a farmer for much needed food, but I begged her to keep them. She finally gave them to me. Now I felt good wearing them, walking beside a handsome young man.

By now, we got into the spirit of the evening. The taxi stopped at the main entrance to the Park Hotel. A uniformed bellboy rushed over and opened the door.

"Good evening, Madam. Welcome to the Park Hotel," he said. James paid the cab driver. He grinned and took my arm. We were beginning to have fun.

We were ushered to a table for two that overlooked the park. What a treat it was in these still chaotic times to sit down at a table covered with a white damask tablecloth and real damask napkins, set with real china and crystal glasses.

I looked around the room. There were two or three older couples who obviously belonged there, like my parents before the war. Others looked as if they did not fit in. The women wore too much makeup and gaudy jewelry, and they talked too loud. The men drank too much, pulled out bulging wallets and did not show good table manners. Rumors circulated that people like these had made their money on the black market and then showed off their new riches, and their bad manners. Later that evening, James told me about the carpetbaggers in the Civil War and how these people reminded him of them.

James spoke some German, but not very well. He wanted to learn, but I was so determined to still improve my English that I probably did not give him enough chance to become fluent. I helped him read the menu, and he was able to order by himself. We decided to try the beef *rouladen*, filled meat rolls, and *spaetzle*, a regional dumpling. Since James seemed to have a little trouble reading the German wine list, the waiter suggested a wine to accompany the meal. Remembering my parents' pre-war dinners, though, I had already picked one of the native *Uhlbach* wines.

"Excellent choice, Madam," the waiter said approvingly, "excellent choice."

It had been a very long time since I had a meal as delicious as this. I loved everything, and so did James. When the band started to play, he asked me to dance. My friends and I always laughed when we saw Americans dance, so clumsy and different from our dances. At least, this is what it looked like to us. James had taken me to the American Club a few times where a German band played. He soon mastered a tango, foxtrot and slow waltz. In turn, he taught me the American swing dance. As hard as he tried, he never managed a real waltz.

"The men are looking at you," he whispered into my ear as we were gliding easily across the dance floor.

"No," I giggled, "it is the women who are looking at you."

The evening ended too soon. Our waiter offered to call a cab, but we convinced him that it was too beautiful a night to be riding in a car and that we would rather walk. Of course, the real reason for the refusal was that the evening had just about depleted our finances.

"Madam," James said as he linked my arm through his, "our carriages await us at the train station."

It was a beautiful starlit night, and in no time at all we reached the train station. James caught a shuttle bus back to the barracks while I took a streetcar to my humble abode. It was a very small, furnished, unheated room in an attic of a house that belonged to some of my parents' old friends. Only part of the house was still standing, but I was lucky to have been offered this place. Housing was almost impossible to find in the destroyed city. Before we parted, we decided to repeat the evening before too long.

The next morning we passed in the hall and James winked at me. And of course, there was that mischievous grin.

One of my colleagues who walked next to me casually said, "You two must have had a big night last night."

"Indeed, we did," I answered. "We had a very big night." When I saw the shocked expression on the woman's face, I laughed out loud. "No, not that kind of night," I replied and giggled at the puzzled look on her face.

We went back to the Park Hotel as often as our finances would allow. Sometimes, I wore a borrowed light green wool dress, sometimes a gray-striped suit; but the green satin dress was my favorite. Margit finally gave it to me.

Usually, we were seated at the same table overlooking the park, and the same waiter waited on us. James, with his charm, easy smile and impeccable manners, soon endeared himself to the staff. One day, he sent his compliments to the chef who came out to talk with him, and they actually discussed his grandmothers' Eastern European recipes. On our fourth or fifth visit, the manager came over to greet us. By now, James was Mr. James, and everyone knew him.

"Mr. James, you here in Deutschland for studies?" the manager inquired in his best English. I cringed when I saw the grin appear on James's face, not knowing what his reply would be.

"Yes sir, and to learn the German language."

The man nodded, then turned to me with a questioning look. "And Madam?"

Before I could utter a word, James said, "Oh, she is here to do literary research. Since she speaks fluent German, she was selected for this project."

The man's eyes widened with a look of deep respect. "For a book or movie?'

"Something like that," James responded. Everyone was impressed and treated us like royalty every time we visited.

"I can't believe you said this," I scolded him after we left the hotel that night.

"I can't either," he laughed. It was the only fib I ever caught him in. He extended his arm to me, "Madam, may I invite you for an evening stroll in the moonlight around the lake in the park?"

"Mr. James, I would be delighted to accept your invitation," I laughed, taking his arm. Life was good. My war-torn soul was beginning to heal.

Our town excursions and history lessons continued. Stuttgart is a wine-growing area, and one of its unique features are the vineyards in the middle of town. Some vineyards are planted all the way down to the asphalt roads. No other city can boast of this. Orchards and vineyards are on the hills surrounding the town and spread down to the Neckar River. The first documentation of wine-growing goes back to the year 1108. Wine-growing was the main industry until the nineteenth century.

Other unique features in my town are the mineral springs, the largest in Europe after Budapest, Hungary. When I suggested to go swimming at Bad Berg early one morning after night shift, before most people got up, James thought my idea was crazy. Still, he came along; and after his first visit, he loved it.

The mineral waters were discovered by the Romans who bathed there. Bad Berg is the oldest swimming pool in Stuttgart. It was established in 1856 by the royal gardener Friedrich Neuner. Therefore, the pool often is still called "The Neuner." The water flow is very brisk, and because of this the water temperature in both the inside and the outside pool is around seventy-six to seventy-eight degrees. No chemicals need to be added. I have been swimming all my life, and a cold-water pool never bothered me.

Sometimes, some of the others who worked night shift accompanied us. We dove into the cool water and swam to the middle of the large pool, nearly as large as a small lake. There, the spring water comes up directly from the ground, and a drinking fountain was set up. We swam to the fountain and stopped for a drink, then swam to the other end of the pool and back, laughing and splashing and racing each other. We collapsed at the end of the pool and stretched out on blankets to dry off in the sun and to take a nap for an hour or two. There were no former enemies, just a group of young people with a zest for life, having fun. Today, when I go back to visit my hometown, I still go to Bad Berg. There is a heated indoor pool now, but I am still a strong swimmer and prefer to swim across the outdoor pool and back, recalling those happy summer days.

One other place where someone could drink mineral water was at the Kursaal in the Kurpark, once a spa in nearby Bad Cannstatt. It was a grandiose building, started in 1825 and completed in 1841. Kings and queens from many countries came to bathe in the healing waters in the park. An air raid in 1943 destroyed the building. It burned to the ground. It was rebuilt in 1949 and now looks like a castle. It is used mostly for meetings, conferences and festivals. There are fountains in the courtyard where a person can sit in leisure and drink mineral waters. James and I went there one time, just to admire the building and grounds, but we thought it was much more fun to drink mineral water from the fountain at the Bad Berg pool.

One sunny spring day in 1939, just a few months before World War II started, I stood in the street with many other people. Above us floated a *zeppelin*, a large airship constructed by Count Ferdinand von Zeppelin, announcing the opening of the horticulture show at the Killesberg Park, north of the center of the town. Beautiful gardens were created with exotic flowers, plants and trees. A small train with open carriages wound its way through the park. At the beginning of the war, the park closed. It suffered extensive damage during the bombings of Stuttgart. It was brought back into operation in 1949.

James and I visited the park several times, but instead of taking the train, we liked to ride the chairlift and enjoy the view from above. Today, the park has expanded and is home to many exhibits during the year. There also is a conference hall, a swimming pool and an observation tower.

Not all of the Killesberg history is good history. Stuttgart was home to many Jews who had lived there for generations. In 1941 and 1942, about one thousand Jews were rounded up and brought to the Killesberg. From there, they were taken to the train station and deported to concentration camps. One of my grandpa's best friends and his family were among them.

Southwest of the Killesberg and not too far from the park is the Bismarck Turm, a tower commemorating the German chancellor Otto von Bismarck. The building of the tower was financed completely by students of the Technical University in Stuttgart. They raised funds and collected donations. The building was completed in 1901. On top of the tower was a "fire bowl," which was used to light fires for midsummer solstice celebrations. When the tower fell in bad repair, it was closed for several years during the 1950s. James and I could never climb to the top of it, but the view of the city from the bottom of the tower was still stunning. The tower reopened for the public again in 2002.

Another important tower in the city is the Tagblatt Turm. The eighteen-story building on Eberhard Street was completed in 1928. It was labeled one of the first skyscrapers in Germany. It received its name from the newspaper *Tagblatt*, that was published there for many years. All buildings around the tower were completely destroyed, but miraculously, the Tagblatt Turm was not hit by bombs and did not burn. Even the paternoster, the moving elevator, was still working during the hours when power was available.

Since it was one of the few remaining buildings still standing, American forces occupied it in 1945 and published the first information leaflets for the population. In September 1945, the large Stuttgart newspaper *Stuttgarter Zeitung* started publishing from the tower. They stayed there until 1978 when they moved to larger quarters. Today the tower houses several theaters and designer stores.

Stuttgart also has of one of the most beautiful botanical gardens and zoos, the Wilhelma. In 1842, King Wilhelm I of Wuerttemberg built a Moorish bathhouse designed in Arabian architecture. By 1853, gardens with exotic plants were surrounding the bath house. Then a zoo was added. During World War II, much of this place was destroyed and many animals were killed. Rebuilding was slow, but today the Wilhelma is worth visiting again. There are about nine thousand animals in the zoo, including a monkey house, a bird sanctuary, a bear facility and a petting zoo. James and I visited several times, admiring the lush growth of unusual plants and the nearly magical water lilies and lotus ponds.

We also visited most of the restored and reopened museums. My favorite as a child was the Museum of Natural History, and it still is. I was fascinated by the huge dinosaur skeletons and the fossils embedded in amber. Fortunately, some of the museum's treasures were removed to safe places before the heavy bombing started. Still, much was destroyed. The museum was reopened in another part of the city very shortly after James left. I regretted that I was not able to show him this part of my childhood.

From all the museums we visited, James liked the Linden Museum best. It also received heavy damage, mostly from fire in the war. Much of it was restored, and it displayed my favorite exhibit of the Indians of North America again. James, of course, knew their history well. Here, he became the teacher, introducing me to the early culture of America's native inhabitants. Today, Africa, Asia, the Orient and others are included in the exhibits.

In the southwest of the town is the *Birkenkopf*, the highest hill within the city. One day, we took a streetcar to the *Botnanger Sattel*, then walked on a footpath through the forest. Visitors always marvel about how well the forests are kept and how clean they are. After a ten-minute walk, we reached the *Birkenkopf*. The people of Stuttgart call the place *Monte Scherbelino*, the Mound of Shards. When the cleanup in the city began after the war, debris and broken stones of the destroyed city were carted to this hill. Originally, the hill was 471 meters (1,545 ft.) high. It grew to 511 meters (1,677 ft.).

A huge American car was parked in the small parking area at the bottom of the hill. When we reached the top, several people were looking out over the city, admiring the view. Looking to the east, one could see the Neckar River, to the south were the distant hills of the *Schwaebische Alb*; and on very clear days even parts of the Black Forest could be seen. James was proud that he now recognized many of the landmarks and buildings. A young couple stood near us. After a while, they came over and asked James if they could join us. They did not speak German and were very impressed with his knowledge of the town, and James loved being the tour guide for a change.

"Where did you learn this?" the man wanted to know.

"I have a good teacher," James grinned, as he put his arm around my waist.

On the very top of the mound was a wooden cross. Close by, in the middle of debris and broken stones, was a plaque with these words engraved on it: "This mound was erected after World War II from the debris of the destroyed city of Stuttgart as a memorial to the dead and a warning to the living."

We stayed about an hour; then we all went down the hill together. The huge car belonged to the young couple, and they offered to give us a ride downtown. We declined; we would rather walk back through the forest and catch a streetcar. As we said goodbye, the man turned around and looked up at the cross.

"Looking at this I see and feel for the first time how senseless and futile all wars are," he said.

The wooden cross was replaced by a steel cross in 2003. Every year on Easter morning there is an Easter sunrise service on top of the hill. The cross reminds us that even though we had abandoned the Lord, He never abandoned us. He was always there.

I think one of the most unique customs in my hometown is the *Kehrwoche*. It is not only a Swabian custom but a law that dates back several hundred years. It is observed not only in the city but everywhere in the State of Wuerttemberg. Literally translated, *Kehrwoche* means "sweeping week." I was so used to seeing women on Saturdays sweep in front of their houses and in the street, that I did not realize how strange this custom must have looked to someone from outside the state, not to mention from another continent. James noticed it, and one day, he asked me about it.

Kehrwoche was instituted by Count Eberhard the Bearded in 1492 as a city ordinance. Stuttgart at that time had a population of nearly seven thousand people. According to this law, each citizen had to clean up around his property at least every two weeks or pay a fine.

Today, *Kehrwoche* is automatically included in contracts for apartment rentals. There is the little *Kehrwoche* and the big *Kehrwoche*. Residents have to take turns fulfilling this law. The little *Kehrwoche* is observed every day by sweeping and wet-mopping the inside stairwells and hallways. The big *Kehrwoche* takes place on Saturdays and requires sweeping in front of the house and in the street. It also includes snow removal from the sidewalks in wintertime, a stipulation which must be completed no later than eight o'clock in the morning, or the residents would pay a fine. *Kehrwoche* is one reason that Swabian cities are so clean.

One evening, we stopped at the lake in the park to feed the swans.

James said, "I received my orders today. I will return to the States in a week."

For a second, my heart stopped beating. I knew that this time would come. I also knew that James was looking forward to going home to see his family, especially his mother, and to embark on his future. He had so many ambitious plans. He talked about them often. First, he would go to law school. He would become the best attorney the country had ever seen. He would eventually be rich, rich enough to buy a beautiful home for his mother and hire a maid for her. He would buy a car. Not one of the *Strassenkreuzer*, the street cruisers, American soldiers had here. He wanted a German Mercedes, manufactured right here in Stuttgart.

The week went by fast, much too fast. We worked one more night shift together, and then I took a few days of vacation. We spent afternoons and evenings walking in the city, visiting some favorite places one more time.

We went to see a new exhibit at the art gallery, and we sat in open air cafés drinking coffee or mineral water, eating ice cream. Ice cream was something that just recently had become available again. James told me about the many different ice cream flavors they had in America. Here, a customer could only get chocolate or vanilla flavors. We stood on the restored Neckar Bridge and watched boats float down the river, and we sat in the afternoon sun in Castle Square.

One afternoon, I took him to a church we had not visited before, St. Elisabeth, only a couple of blocks from where I grew up. The church tower had received a direct hit from a bomb, but the clock never stopped running nor chiming. When our Lutheran St. Paulus Church was destroyed, the Catholic St. Elisabeth Church let the Lutheran congregation hold their services there for a while until St. Elisabeth also was damaged.

I never attended a service at St. Elisabeth. As I grew

up, my friends and I were too busy with other Sunday activities planned by our teachers and Hitler Youth leaders. We went to see political or historical movies; we had lots of sports activities; and we attended lectures and seminars. Still, I was very familiar with St. Elisabeth. One of my best friends was Catholic, and her family was a member of St. Elisabeth. As children, we walked to school together many times. Her family stopped at the church for prayer often, and her mother expected her to stop for prayer on her way to school.

Unknown to my very strict Lutheran family, I accompanied her often. I loved the beautiful stained-glass windows, the glowing candles, the statues of the Virgin Mary and of saints whose names I did not know. I always felt good coming here. James, who once told me that he was raised as a Catholic, was surprised by the beautiful interior of the restored church. He also seemed a little surprised that I was so at ease with the custom of dipping my fingertips in the holy water and crossing myself.

We slipped into a pew and knelt. After a while, James got up and went to the front. He put some money in a beautiful wood-carved box and picked up two candles. He carefully lit them and placed them with the other candles. He stood for a while, and I wondered if he was praying. We never talked about our different religions; in fact, we never discussed our faith. Religion was not an important part in my life, nor in the lives of my friends. The war had made it impossible to believe in God. Hitler had accomplished that much. Yet, at this moment, kneeling in this church, I felt strangely at peace.

On the evening before James left, we went to the Park Hotel for one last meal. James wore his borrowed black suit, and I wore my green satin dress. The evening was bittersweet. James told everyone he had to go back to

America to finish his studies, and I too would be leaving as soon as I finished the last of my research. They all presumed that I also was American, and we never corrected them. Everyone came to bid us goodbye and to wish us well. James left an extra-large tip for our favorite waiter. There was no band that night, no last dance.

"Madam," the manager said, "you will come back before you leave?" I promised, knowing that this was a promise I would not keep.

I did go back to the Park Hotel one more time, about twenty-five years later. During one of my visits, my father took me there for dinner one evening. The elegant furnishings looked the same. There was still a table for two overlooking the park, but I asked not to be seated by the window.

The clientele had changed from the early 1950s. There were no over-dressed, over-jeweled women with too much makeup; no men showing off their bulging billfolds. The atmosphere was quiet and dignified. I did not recognize any of the staff. I asked about the manager who was there when James and I came to the hotel. He had retired and died a few years ago. The chef left when a new manager took over, and nobody remembered our favorite waiter.

My father and I soon realized that we had made a mistake in coming here. He conjured up the image of a black-haired woman in a red silk dress, and I was thinking of a young man in a borrowed suit with a mischievous grin. Both were gone forever. In 2006, the Park Hotel was torn down to make room for the Southwest Radio Network. Another part of my town's history disappeared, this time not by the destruction of war, but by what is called progress.

It was James who suggested afterwards that we go to the tower. This place was the first one that I had brought him to, and he wanted to look out over the city one last time. We quietly stood by the railing and watched the lights below. There were still dark spots, but not as many as the first time we were here. We stood silently for a long time. Finally, James turned around and put his arm around my waist.

"Thank you," he said.

"For what?" I asked.

"For sharing your beautiful city with me, for making me see her through your eyes."

"Thank you too," I whispered, "for the sunshine days you gave me."

His lips slowly touched mine, not in one of the fun friendship kisses we had exchanged so easily, but in a long, lingering kiss that turned into a passionate embrace.

The mood was scattered in a minute. A tower guard clattered up the stairs and noisily threw open the door to the balcony.

"Hey, you love birds," he hollered, "the tower will close in thirty minutes."

"Will you come to the train tomorrow when I leave?" James asked. I shook my head.

A few months before, a friend had asked me to accompany her to the station when her boyfriend returned to the U.S. The place was pandemonium. The platform was filled with soldiers waiting to board a troop train. Most of them were happy to be returning home.

But there were the German girlfriends, some of them with babies in their arms. The GI boyfriends kissed their crying girlfriends goodbye; the GI daddies kissed their babies, most of them probably for the last time. Many left without a thought about the girls they left behind who now had to struggle for themselves and for their babies.

These girls were shunned often by their own families

and nearly always by the German society. In the early 1950s, many Germans, especially German men, still felt hostile toward Americans. Never mind that these girls often saved whole families from starvation after the war by dating "Ami boys" who gave them food to eat or cigarettes to trade on the black market for the most urgent necessities. Now, they were on their own with uncertain futures for themselves and for their babies. I did not want to say goodbye to James in such surroundings.

"No," I said, swallowing through a tiny lump in my throat. "I will be here on the tower tomorrow to see your train leave." James nodded.

The next morning, I saw the army busses drive up in front of the station and the soldiers, carrying their duffle bags, disembarked. I could not pick out James; the distance between us was too great. About half an hour later, the train came out from the station, winding its way through what seemed hopelessly entangled tracks, then found its way toward the Cannstatt tunnel. I heard the shrill sound of the steam whistle as the train entered the tunnel, and then the red backlights disappeared. I looked up. The sun was covered by clouds. Today would not be a sunshine day. Somehow, I knew I would never see him again.

A few letters came. James was settling in back home, starting law school soon. He offered to find a sponsor for me so that I could work there with my pediatric nursing degree, if I was interested.

I missed him fiercely for a while. We had such an easy, comfortable friendship that is hard to describe, and I missed it. I missed our talks, our long walks, having a cup of coffee together during night shift. I missed his smile when we passed in the hall. Then, a most incredible, nearly unbelievable thing happened. One evening after work, my friend Margit and I stopped at a small sandwich place downtown. The door opened and a man walked in. He stood on the threshold for a few seconds and looked around, and in an instant my life changed forever.

In the early 1960s, several of my former colleagues went to New York to work. We all stayed in touch. In 1961, James and a friend went to New York on business. While there, they met the girls for coffee one afternoon. One of them wrote a letter two weeks before the pre-arranged coffee date and said that James was looking for me. By that time, I was married, had two little children and lived on a military post in Texas.

I was surprised to hear later that James did not stay in law school. He had been so passionate about his dream of becoming an attorney and so sure of what he wanted to do. He had dropped out of school to pursue other business ventures. They paid off, and he became a wealthy man.

James dreamed the American dream, and now he lives it. He is rich, very rich. He has everything materially that he ever wanted. I followed his career off and on over the years, and I am happy for him. I do wonder if he is truly happy with the life he chose. I wish for him that he is.

Our lives are worlds apart. He lives in a guarded mansion and is still tied down by heavy responsibilities. He must live in accordance with the laws of the rich, laws which often restrict and dictate a person's movements and freedom. Sometimes, I wonder if he ever longs for the simplicity of our youth, to be free to walk in a park, to feed the swans and watch a lizard sunning himself or run, laughing, through a cloud burst. Does he sometimes too feel a tiny lingering sadness for carefree days that cannot be recaptured?

Many years have passed since a young woman with auburn hair introduced a young American soldier to her hometown. Many changes have taken place since then, not only in Europe and America, but around the world. James told me about his country, and today this America he talked about with such fierce pride is now also my country. It is the country I love, where I raised my children, where my grandchildren grew up and where my great-grandchildren will have their future.

Occasionally, I go back to Stuttgart. It took twenty-two years after the war until the city was completely rebuilt, and the scars from the war were covered. Some of the old historical buildings were restored, and some were razed and replaced with modern and ultra-modern structures. Much of what I knew and loved has changed or is gone. But it is still my town, the town where I was born and grew up, the town I will always love.

I have many memories, good ones and bad ones. When I visit, I always go to the tower where James and I had often looked over the beautiful city that stretches from the forested hills down to the Neckar River. I go alone. He is the only person that I ever shared this place with.

I see the changes that have happened and are still happening. Construction and building is always going on somewhere in the city. The train station is supposed to be moved underground; the tracks will not be visible from above anymore. Nobody will see the trains from the faraway places coming in and going out of the station. The tower will still be there, but everything around it will change. They call it Stuttgart 21. The city fathers are trying to keep up with "progress."

I have followed James' success off and on over the years. The Internet now makes this process easy. Occasionally, I find a photo of him on the Internet. His black curls have turned gray. He still looks good in exquisitely-tailored suits; and in one photo, I thought I detected just a hint of that old, mischievous grin. I know that I will never see him again, but he will always hold a tiny piece of my heart because he brought sunshine and healing to my war-torn soul.

My grandpa's Bible and I
2007

THE BIBLE

Published in 1686 by Johann Andreas Endters of Nuernberg, Germany

Nobody knows who the first owner of the Bible was. Since it was published in Nuernberg, it could have belonged to one of the rich merchants living there, or to an earl or count or some other member of German nobility. The custom of these families was often to gather the entire household, including the servants, every evening for a devotion. The head of the household read from a Bible, followed by prayer. The Bible also could have been an "altar Bible," a Bible that was kept at the altar of a large church or cathedral for Sunday services. The average citizen could not afford such a valuable book even if he could read. A twenty-two-pound Bible with ornate brass moldings, covered in white leather pigskin, would have been an untouchable rarity.

The Bible belonged to my grandfather's friend Mr. Neff, who lived in one of Stuttgart's suburbs. Grandpa also had an old Bible printed only a few years later. Before Hitler became the leader of Germany, they compared their Bibles often. They found that they were nearly the same, except for the description of the city of Jerusalem, a map of the travel routes of the Israelites, images of some of the prophets and, most of all, the unusual description of Noah's Ark in Mr. Neff's Bible.

The two families attended church together for many years. After having lost nearly everything during the bombings of Stuttgart, my grandparents moved to their little house in the country. More than 60% of the city was destroyed. Miraculously, Mr. Neff's house was spared. The Bible also was spared from the sweeping destruction of religious artifacts that took place during Adolf Hitler's regime.

After the war, my grandparents stayed in touch with their old church the best they could. About every other month, they undertook the arduous trip to Stuttgart, part of the way by bus, part by train and part on foot, just to attend services. When Mr. Neff died, they went to his funeral.

Mr. Neff had one child, a son who was confirmed with me. Confirmation is a public profession of faith for young teens in many protestant churches, as well as in the Catholic church. It requires at least one year of instructions and study of the Bible. Neither one of us wanted to go through this ceremony, but we were forced by our families to comply. Like so many young people at that time, Mr. Neff's son had renounced all his Lutheran faith and its teaching. After the funeral, people gathered at Mr. Neff's house.

"What happened to your father's Bible?" my grandfather asked the young man.

"Oh," he answered, "it is in the attic. If you want it you better get it right now, because I am either going to throw it in the trash or burn it."

My grandfather, a slender, undernourished man in those days of starvation, climbed up into the attic. After rummaging around for a while he found the Bible. He carried it downstairs and made sure again that he could keep it. I am not sure how he and Grandma managed to carry the heavy twenty-two-pound Bible to the train, then to the bus and finally a short walk to their home. Grandma took off her coat, wrapped the Bible in it; and each of them carried one end of the coat.

Even though Grandpa's eyesight had declined, he could still read the old Bible. After Grandma's death, the book became an even more powerful source of strength for him. He always told me that he wanted me to have the Bible after his death, but I had to promise that I would not sell it to make a profit. Even though I encountered hard financial times in my life, I kept the promise.

I was living in America when Grandpa died in 1967. I was not able to go to his funeral. Several people from his old church attended the funeral, and someone remembered the Bible. They wanted it. Nobody had wanted it when Grandpa climbed into the attic and saved it from certain destruction. Someone mentioned that it was probably valuable now and would bring a nice sum of money. There were heated arguments. Then, one old lady remembered that Grandpa mentioned several times that the book should be given to his granddaughter.

My girlfriend and my father collected the Bible and brought it to Stuttgart. I received a letter stating that the Bible would be mailed to me. They carefully sealed it in a plastic bag, packed it in a sturdy box and took it to the post office. The postmaster refused to accept it. He said it was too valuable and could not be insured for shipping to America. My girlfriend sent another letter, informing me about this. She did not say what would happen to the Bible, but I presumed that someone in Grandpa's church would sell it after all.

About three months later, the mail carrier brought a large box to my door, labeled "old books." Neither the German nor the American customs offices had examined the contents. It was shipped by book rate and traveled nearly eight weeks across the ocean. My grandpa's Bible had arrived in America.

I treasured Grandpa's gift for many years but only opened it a few times to admire the drawings by Joseph Fuerttenbach. Then one day, I had to leave my home suddenly under dire circumstances and left the Bible as well as my library of books and most everything else that I owned behind. Most of my books were viciously destroyed. The Bible was found several years later in my old home on the floor of a walk-in-closet, unprotected, but still in good shape. One of my sons picked it up, and wrapped it in a black trash bag. He gave it to my other son to bring it to me in North Carolina. On the trip to North Carolina, my son spent the night in a motel in a small town. Not realizing the value of the book, he left it unprotected in the back of his pickup. Incredibly, nobody took it.

I do not know what other trials the Bible went through before it came into the hands of Mr. Neff, who had apparently bought it in a secondhand bookstore in the late 1920s. Why did the original owner or his children not keep it? These questions are unanswered. The fact is that the Bible was protected and had survived. In 2007, I donated the Bible to Mars Hill University, a small Baptist university in North Carolina. The Bible is now restored and on display in the Renfro Library at Mars Hill University.

THE MEMORIAL
Stuttgart 1997

During a visit in Stuttgart in May 1997, I spent one afternoon at the *Lapidarium* in the *Stiftsfruchtkasten* on Schiller Square, researching one of my ancestors. I was looking for a Roman stone from the mid-second century that was found in Murrhardt in 1675. The stone was dedicated to the sun god Mithras by a member of the 24th Cohort of Roman volunteers.

A relative told me that our ancestor's brother found the stone in the creek behind his mill, dug it out and used it for a cornerstone of his house. Two hundred years later, the stone was removed from his house and taken to the Roman *Lapidarium* in Stuttgart. The curator was not very familiar with the story, but he allowed me to do my own search in the building.

Just as I located the stone in the very back of the room, an elderly couple entered. They asked the curator something in English, then in very broken German. They obviously could not communicate; so I made my way to the front and offered my help to translate.

The couple, tourists from New York, were looking for the Jewish synagogue. The curator produced a telephone book, and the man wrote down the address. He had a city map, and we helped him find the exact location. They both thanked us and assured us that they would be able to find it. They turned to leave; and at the spur of the moment, I asked them if I could show them something very close by. Just around the corner was a memorial for people killed during the Nazi regime (*Mahnmal fuer die Opfer des Nationalsozialismus*).

On the way there, I explained the memorial. It was designed by Elmar Daucher and consists of four very large stone blocks, made of black granite from Brazil. Three blocks hold up one block above, with an entrance at the front. We slowly entered the memorial. A flower bouquet lay on the floor, next to a plaque with these words inscribed on it: "*Verfemt, verstossen, gemartert, erschlagen, erhaengt, vergast - Millionen Opfer der nationalsozialistischen Gewaltsherrschaft beschwoeren Dich: niemals wieder.*"

I quietly translated. It was not easy: "Proscribed, rejected, tortured, slain, hung, gassed—millions of victims of the national socialism tyranny beseech you: never again."

The lady put both hands on the granite stones; tears streamed down both our faces. Her husband, overcome by feelings, had already backed out. Once outside, the woman told me that they had lived all their lives in New York. Their families went back for generations in that area. They never had relatives in Germany, had not lost anyone in the Holocaust; but she had harbored a terrible hate against all

German people. Her husband had wanted to visit Germany since the end of the war, but she refused to go.

Finally, in the autumn of their lives, she decided to grant him this wish; and she accompanied him to Germany. She was surprised to find kind, generous and helpful people, not at all what she had expected. She suddenly realized that many of them had also suffered a great deal under the Nazi regime. Many had lost their whole families and everything they owned during the bombings of the German cities. Her attitude started to change; her hate left.

"And then," she said, "I meet a wonderful woman like you." We stood there for a while, holding hands, while her husband took some photos. Still crying, she hugged me tight, and whispered, "Thank you for bringing us here." Only after they had left did I realize that we never exchanged names.

Elfriede E. Wilde

CHAPTER FOUR

TEXAS

The taillights of the big Greyhound bus disappeared around a bend in the road. It was four o'clock in the morning on a humid November day in 1957. I had arrived in Texas, my new home. The air was warm and damp and smelled of rain. Daylight would be here soon. Even though the November night was much warmer than the cold nights in Germany, I stood shivering on the wooden porch of a country store, two suitcases and two airline bags beside me. My husband and I had decided to travel light. The rest of our belongings would arrive a few weeks later.

I looked at my surroundings in the dim streetlight. The sign on the building behind me read *General Store*. The wooden porch extended in front of several buildings along the street. It seemed to be the town's main shopping area. About two blocks down the street, I could see the lights of a gas station into which my husband had just disappeared. He remembered that this place was open all night, and he could use their phone to call a taxi to take us to his mother's house several miles out of town.

I was born and raised in a large European city. This sleepy little Texas town looked just about like one of those I had seen in Western movies. Standing on the wooden porch alone, I nearly expected to see a cowboy coming around the corner, wielding a pistol, or a rider racing down the street, shooting. For a moment, I wondered why I had left my home and come to this strange, frightening place.

My thoughts went back to the last few years. After I returned from Scotland, I made plans to work for family friends in Paris, France. But I fell in love with a dark-haired, blue-eyed Texas farm boy. I was ready to follow him to the end of the world, and now it looked like I had.

The last few months at home passed quickly. Friends and relatives stopped by to bring gifts to take to my new home. They were treasures that had survived the bombings. One relative had five small photos of my father from before the war, the only ones that still existed. My great-aunt brought one of my mother's paintings, and another relative gave me my great-grandmother's copper cake pan.

On the morning that we boarded a train to Frankfurt, a few friends came to see us off. Everyone was crying, everyone but me. I was far too excited and eager to embark on a new life with the man I loved.

The next morning, a sunny Sunday morning, we boarded a plane to New York in the Frankfurt airport. At 10:00 a.m., we swept over the Autobahn, granting me a last glimpse of Germany. Eighteen hours later, after a stop in Newfoundland, we circled over New York. The sight was unforgettable. As we descended, I saw miles and miles of lights, as if a huge carnival had just arrived. In the 1950s, things were quiet in Germany on a Sunday night. This city was alive.

For the next three days, I joined a group of women I had befriended on the plane. While our husbands were reporting to a military station for processing, we explored New York. We looked at skyscrapers, went to the top of the Empire State building, rode under the Hudson River in a car and walked across Times Square. The only other city of this size that I had seen was London. My hometown, considered a large city in Germany, seemed small compared to this city. Since then, I have been to New York several times, and it still is a most fascinating place to visit.

The trip south on a Greyhound bus was another new

experience for me. First came the toll bridge out of New York. All vehicles had to pay a fee to be allowed to cross the bridge. We stopped at Baltimore and Washington, D.C. I would have liked to see more of these cities but had to wait years before I could.

People got on and off the bus. Their accents changed the further south we drove. I gained a host of new impressions—different scenery, food at the travel stops that I had never tasted before, and women's fashion that was more casual than in Europe. I hardly slept, trying to take it all in.

Across the aisle from us sat two women, obviously friends. One was white, the other black. I don't remember what town it was when the black lady was not allowed to enter the same dining room as the rest of us. Her white friend complained to no avail. They got off the bus at the next stop and decided to rent a car to reach their destination. I wondered why this took place. It brought back memories of my mother and Irmgard, one of her Jewish childhood friends. After Hitler became the chancellor of Germany, Irmgard and her family were not allowed to eat or shop in non-Jewish establishments anymore.

In just a few minutes that seemed like an hour, my husband returned. A taxi would be here shortly. Soon a car drove up, and a man wearing the biggest cowboy hat I had ever seen leaned out the window.

"Howdy," he yelled. "Are you the people who called me?"

A long conversation followed about what road to take to my mother-in-law's home. It had rained hard the day before, and some of the dirt roads were flooded. We had to take the "long way" around. I had no idea what a dirt road was. During our drive, the man asked me several times if I really was from Europe. He stared at me as if he expected me to have two heads or four arms.

A faint glow of daylight rose in the east. We passed fields with still unharvested crops and with pine trees, looking much different from German pine trees. Finally, the car drove down a small, sandy road. Two houses came in sight, cars parked in front of one of them. People spilled out, greeting us. Trixie, our little dog that we had shipped ahead to Texas, jumped into my arms. It was total confusion. Then, I found myself sitting at a large round table, loaded with a Texas breakfast. There were fried eggs, bacon, sausage, homemade biscuits with homemade butter, cereal and several preserves. In Germany, the usual breakfast was coffee, a slice or two of bread with butter and jelly and maybe a hard-boiled egg. Suddenly, I realized how hungry I was. I had been told in Germany that many people in America prayed before meals. I was relieved that nobody did. I also was afraid that I would be asked to go to church on Sunday with my mother-in-law's family, but nobody went to church.

People asked me questions, usually not even waiting for an answer, and I still did not know who everyone was. Then, the long travel took its toll, and I became very tired. Gratefully, I accepted the offer to take a bath. I ran hot water into the tub, looking forward to relaxing. As I was undressing, there was a knock at the door.

"Mom said to shut off the water," my sister-in-law called. "We don't have water here like oil." I looked at the two inches of water in the tub, drained it and washed my face and hands at the sink.

Something awoke me from a deep sleep. There was a dreadful smell. My husband was snoring softly beside me. Then I saw Trixie cuddled up between us. She emitted a horrible odor. A closer examination revealed that her back was covered with cow manure.

Trixie also had found new things in this country and had delighted in playing in the pasture close to the house, rolling herself in grass and manure. How would I ever be able to get her clean in this place where apparently oil was more plentiful than water? I had much to learn in this new land. Not wanting to use my mother-in-law's towels, I wet one of our towels I had packed in my suitcase and rubbed Trixie clean the best I could. Then I doused her with cologne. We all had to wait to take a full bath until we had our own place again.

On the second day of our visit, I was convinced that my mother-in-law was very ill. She spit blood, or so it seemed. I was afraid she had tuberculosis, an illness much feared in post-war Germany. My husband informed me that she was chewing and spitting chewing tobacco. I had much to learn about this land that was to become my home.

A few days later, we bought a car and headed south to Fort Hood, my husband's new military station. The land looked different. The vastness of the country was overwhelming, nearly frightening. Sometimes we drove for miles, passing a farm house occasionally. Most people seemed to live in cities. There were few trees, some of which I had never seen. The landscape was dotted with oil wells that looked like large vultures digging their huge beaks into the ground. At night, the stars in the Texas sky were brighter and more brilliant than I had ever seen, sparkling like millions of diamonds thrown across the universe by an unseen hand.

The one-story wooden houses painted in rainbow colors looked strange. Their windows were screened. I was told this was to keep out insects and flies. Most homes had no entry halls; one stepped directly into the living room. And doors had round door knobs.

Our first home was a small apartment. The summer was unbearably hot. Nobody had prepared me for Texas summers nor for rattlesnakes in the yard. I also fought a constant battle with sand blown into the house by hot winds.

My mother-in-law visited once for a few days. After she returned home, I heard that she whispered to her neighbors, "she dusts her furniture every day, washes her windows every other week, and she irons my son's underwear. But can you imagine, she does not know how to bake cornbread and has no idea what biscuits are."

I worked to restore my ruined reputation. I stopped dusting every day, forgot to wash windows and one day decided that floors did not have to be so clean that someone could eat off them. Who would want to eat off the floor anyway? I asked a neighbor to teach me the art of making biscuits; and after a while, I was able to produce a biscuit so light that it nearly melted in my mouth. Unfortunately, my mother-in-law, who prided herself to be the best biscuit-maker in the county, was not too thrilled with my newfound skill.

I had no idea what fried okra or black-eyed peas were, and I had never tasted a honeydew melon. I was introduced to drive-in diners where waitresses on roller skates, called car hops, brought hamburgers and fries and root beer floats directly to our car. There was no McDonald's in the area yet. In restaurants, I mistook the glass of water brought to the table for a finger bowl. I had never heard of drinking plain water with a meal. In Germany, we sometimes had wine or beer with meals, or mineral water.

I discovered the Sears and Roebuck catalogue and Betty Crocker's cookbook. I read both as if they were novels, often sitting up late into the night, marveling at the wonders contained therein. I cruised grocery stores with a shopping cart, at first just looking, then touching and finally boldly putting unknown items into the cart. I bought items like cake mixes, pie fillings, turnip greens, honeydew melons and self-rising flour. I read and re-read recipes. I converted grams to ounces, Celsius oven temperatures to Fahrenheit; and I had some major kitchen disasters. Then, I found the perfect solution to some of my cooking problems—canned goods. I was becoming an American.

At times, I was a little homesick. I missed the snow. I longed for a slice of rye bread, and I would have loved to sink my teeth into a sour apple from my grandpa's orchard. But I was becoming an American.

NEHEMIAH

Several years later, we were living in our own small home in the country, a few miles from Fort Hood, Texas. I had two small children, no car, and I was stuck at home most of the time. I missed visiting my old friends and mingling with people. Just down the road from us was a small Baptist church. I had no clue what a Baptist church was. In Germany, most of the churches were either Catholic or Lutheran. On Sundays and even sometimes during the week, I saw children playing in the church yard. My children needed playmates.

I had little money; so I wrote a letter to my father. I told him that I would like to join a women's organization but that everyone there was dressed so nicely, I would feel out of place. I knew he would send money, and he did. Had I told him that I wanted to buy something to wear to attend a church, he would not have sent a penny. He never went to church.

At that time, women wore hats to go to church, so I bought a hat, matching shoes, a purse and gloves that would go with one of my good dresses. The very next Sunday, I dressed my children in their best outfits, and we walked to the church. My husband absolutely refused to go with us. He never went with us to this church during the time we lived there, not even one time.

Everyone was nice and welcomed us. Soon, we started to go every Sunday. My children went to children's classes. They loved it and made friends while I sat in church, not knowing what was going on. I loved the music; but when the preacher talked, I did not know what he was talking about. I was bored. I did not want to be rude and openly look at my watch, so I peeked at it every few minutes and hoped he would come to the "amen" soon.

My children were invited to birthday parties and play dates. I invited people to our house, and some of the women took me shopping. The church had become a place for me to socialize.

And then, something happened. I love to read, especially about history. After a while, I realized that the minister sometimes read and talked about history in the Bible. There were interesting stories. When I went to Scotland in 1950, my paternal grandmother gave me a Bible as a going-away gift. Bibles were available again in German bookstores. It was a useless gift. I had no intention to ever open it, but I kept it because my grandmother had given it to me.

One day, I dug it out and looked up some of the stories I heard about in church. They were fascinating stories, like the story about a young man named David who slew a giant named Goliath with a slingshot. There were stories about real human behavior such as Sarah who became jealous of Hagar and Joseph who was sold by his brothers.

I read them like story books, but I read them. Many of the Proverbs absolutely made sense.

One day, I stumbled onto the book of Nehemiah, a man who was prayerful and persistent. He was rebuilding the destroyed walls of his ancestors' town. I related with this story. My hometown was nearly destroyed during the war, the inner city almost completely gone. It took many, many years to restore it.

Nehemiah also mentioned the word *genealogy*. In chapter 7, he found a register for genealogy, and he listed names. He also listed exact dates and the number of people in families. This list reminded me of the genealogical research we had to do during Hitler's regime. I was impressed. If this story were true, then other stories in the Bible might be true also.

I began to follow the sermons more, and I was beginning to understand them. It was a turning point in my life. I still struggled with the fact that so many of my friends were killed in Germany, that our world was destroyed and that we had lost everything. But finally I was able to accept Jesus and realize that I was a child of God, not a child of the gods. My decision to be baptized by immersion gave me final peace.

Most of my friends in Germany have never accepted this belief. When we talk on the phone, correspond by e-mail or visit in person, I try to tell them about Jesus who loves us, who died for us for our sins. If strangers try to talk to them about God, they become offended and nearly rude. Since we have been lifelong friends, they look at me, then roll their eyes.

"How can you believe this?" they ask. "You were there. We went through bombings, through hell, with death all around us. We went through starvation together. There was no God. We did it ourselves; we dug ourselves out from the rubble with our own hands; and we helped each other to survive. If there had been a God, he would not have let this happen. But there was no God. We did it with our own strength and determination. Don't you remember?"

My heart is sad when I think about the friends I grew up with. They cannot see the amazing love and protection the Lord showered on us to bring us through war and destruction. They cannot see that God was always there, that He never lost sight of us, that He protected and saved us through all the seasons of our lives. I pray that one day they will be able to accept His unconditional love and His amazing grace.

My life here in America was not always easy. My marriage ended in divorce. Then a miracle happened—I found a new husband. He was a kind and gentle man, intelligent, romantic and a great conversationalist. He had a great sense of humor, and we laughed a lot. He was also a Christian. We had happy years together. I will always be thankful that God brought me to this country that even today, with all its problems, is still the greatest country. Here I found Jesus; here I can go to church; and here I can pray without fear.

WORKS CITED

Bardua, Heinz. *Stuttgart im Luftkrieg* (Stuttgart: Stuttgart City Archives, 1985), 144.

Hosseinzadeh, Sonja. *Nur Truemmerfrauen und Ami-Liebchen?* (Tuebingen: Silberburg-Verlag, 1998), 32-33.

Zuern, Max. *Weissach im Tal.* (Auenwald: R. Schlichenmeier, 1980), 320.

About the Author

1943

2015

Elfriede E. Wilde was born in Stuttgart, Germany, three years before Adolf Hitler became the chancellor of the country. She survived the bombings of Stuttgart and the horrors of the war.

After working in Edinburgh, Scotland, for two years after the war she returned to Germany, married a Texas farm boy and came to the United States with him. She retired from the University of Central Arkansas and moved to North Carolina. After the death of her second husband she settled in Texarkana, Texas.

She has published two family history books, numerous genealogy articles and is a member of the Arkansas Genealogy Hall of Fame. She has traveled extensively in Europe and in this continent, experiencing new cultures and making friends around the world.